# *CLASSIC* MEETS
# CONTEMPORARY

# *CLASSIC* MEETS
# CONTEMPORARY

twelve top designers create interiors for today

FLEUR ROSSDALE

INTRODUCED AND SELECTED BY
HENRIETTA SPENCER-CHURCHILL

RIZZOLI
NEW YORK

First published in the United States of America in 1998 by
Rizzoli International Publications, Inc.
300 Park Avenue South, New York, NY 10010

First published in Great Britain in 1998
by Collins & Brown Limited

ISBN 0-8478-2118-8
LC 98-65888

*Editor:* Alexandra Parsons
*Designer:* Christine Wood

Reproduction by Hong Kong Graphic & Printing Ltd
Printed in Hong Kong by Midas Printing Ltd

# CONTENTS

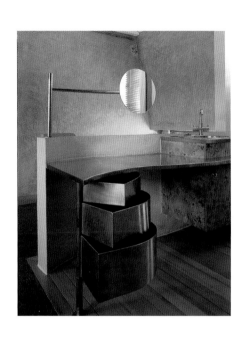

# *FOREWORD*

## by FLEUR ROSSDALE

The British Interior Design Exhibition 1997, held in a magnificent mansion in Cambridge Gate, Regent's Park, London, was the inspiration for this book. The mansion, which was derelict when I began the project, posed an exciting challenge to all the interior designers and architects who I invited to take part. Each designer, twelve of whom are represented in *Classic Meets Contemporary*, brought into being exhilarating interiors.

The Cambridge Gate Exhibition, referred to as The Design House, Cambridge Gate throughout this book, demonstrates an endeavour by all the designers involved to offer enlightenment and inspiration to the public with the aim of encouraging people to take a fresh look at interiors and hopefully inspire them with ideas for their own homes.

*Left* The Design House, Cambridge Gate. The dining room on an upper floor shown prior to decoration.

*Right* Visual by Sibyl Colefax and John Fowler showing their design scheme for the dining room.

*Below* The finished Sibyl Colefax and John Fowler dining room.

# *INTRODUCTION*
## by HENRIETTA SPENCER-CHURCHILL

Creating the right environment in the home is important for our well being and general enjoyment of life. It is also a deeply personal experience, as the result is a physical display of our design skills and ideas for living. Despite these weighty considerations, creating a home should be inspiring, exhilarating and fun. One way to achieve this and ensure rewarding results is to turn to the professionals for help.

### WHY USE AN INTERIOR DESIGNER?
In many areas of life we turn to the help of experts in areas where we may not possess the knowledge or experience to achieve the best results on our own. Indeed, in the process of buying a house we involve numerous professionals – at the very least an estate agent to find the property, a solicitor to deal with the legal documents, an accountant or bank manager to advise on the financing and a surveyor to check the condition of the property. The obvious next step would be to employ a professional interior designer to help make the most of this major investment which is so central to our daily happiness.

There are many good reasons for employing an interior designer, and a few distorted myths about why not to use them. One of the main myths is that bringing in someone else to decide what your home should look like can be considered defeatist, reflecting a lack of personal style. Yet it is hardly a grave admission to realize that you do not have the knowledge and abilities built up over years of experience. Calling in an interior designer can save a great

*Top* Lamp by Christopher Gollut.

*Middle* Table by Charles Rutherfoord.

*Below* Detail of curtain by Jenny Armit, with delicate crystal tie-back by Wendy Cushing Trimmings.

deal of time and effort, not to mention money, because a professional can spot relatively quickly what will and won't work in a space and the best solutions to a problem. A designer will come up with ideas which you are unlikely ever to have thought of simply because you do not possess the same knowledge of design history, decorative techniques, available materials, or supplier contacts.

Another important consideration in this era of ever-increasing time and work pressures is how long it would take you to research, decide, organize and oversee the necessary work involved. An interior designer can take all the hard work out of decorating and leave you with the pleasures of choosing and watching as the changes unfold before you.

THE CLIENT BRIEF

Another fear is that the designer will dominate the proceedings, or that a lack of communication will result in the home ending up as a backdrop to the latest trends and bearing no relation to the clients' lifestyle.

A large part of an interior designer's job, and one of the things which makes it such an exciting field in which to work, is establishing and implementing the client's brief. No two clients are the same and working out exactly what is required is a skill in its own right, particularly when many people have little more than a vague notion of what they want. The designer is there to suggest and interpret for the client. As the interior designers featured in this book clearly demonstrate, each one of them is capable of creating totally different rooms in response to the different clients' desires.

Finally, interior designers are often perceived as an expensive extravagance, yet their expertise can prevent costly mistakes and their practical solutions and ingenious proposals can enhance the value of a property.

*Top* Kitchen created by Charles Bateson Design Consultants.

*Middle* Percheron fabrics used by interior designer Lavinia Dargie.

*Below* Detail of a *trompe l'oeil* ceiling.

# INTRODUCTION

*Below left* Visual by Clifton Interiors for their scheme for the ground floor gentlemen's lavatory at The Design House, Cambridge Gate.

*Below right* The finished ground floor gentlemen's lavatory with fish tank cistern, designed by Clifton Interiors Ltd.

## WHERE TO FIND AN INTERIOR DESIGNER

How do you go about finding an interior designer to suit your needs, whether for a commercial or residential property? There are established professional associations, such as the IIDA and the IDDA, who can supply names and contact numbers for their members. These associations operate rigorous vetting systems and, equally important, operating guidelines. There can, of course, be no better recommendation than that of personal experience, so ask around – maybe even ask if you can speak to previous clients to obtain their opinion.

## SETTING A BUDGET

Charges can vary greatly and there is no set fee so make sure you establish at the outset of a job exactly what you want the designer to do and how much they will charge for the service. You may use them simply in a consultative role, or you may want them to oversee everything from the design, to alteration work and buying furnishings. Always set a budget and work with the designer to remain within this. They will usually come up with ingenious suggestions for achieving the overall effect you desire within budget. Be brave, and you will have the home of your dreams.

*Below left* Colour visual by Clifton Interiors for their scheme for the ground floor ladies' room for The Design House, Cambridge Gate.

*Below right* The ladies' room designed as an 18th-century print room.

# *THE CLASSIC LOOK*

# HENRIETTA SPENCER-CHURCHILL

# THE CLASSIC
# *APPROACH*

*Left* This country house sitting room has been extended to create an extra seating area which benefits from views out over the surrounding landscape.

Brought up in the architectural grandeur of Sir John Vanbrugh and Nicholas Hawksmoor at her family home of Blenheim Palace, Lady Henrietta Spencer-Churchill has an instinctive knowledge of classic English baroque architecture, fine furniture, paintings and sculpture. It therefore comes as no surprise that the classic principles of design, respected and practised for hundreds of years, are paramount in her work as an interior designer. Her rooms tend towards an understated grandeur which creates an ambience of refined comfort. Proportion and a practical use of space are fundamental to her foremost concern of getting the 'bones' of the structural composition correct, allowing the emphasis of architectural details, colour and decoration to follow in natural progression.

## MODERN DAY CLASSICS

This country sitting room (shown left) is typical of an English country farmhouse, with low ceilings yet good overall proportions. It epitomizes Lady Henrietta's ability to combine classical elegance with the simplicity and informality of late 20th-century living. Lady Henrietta extended the room by removing a wall to open up a second seating area. She has then selected and positioned the furniture to create two areas of diverse character; the one formal with antique chairs and upright settee, the other informal with soft sofa and scatter cushions. The two areas are united by the colour scheme picked out from the Oriental rugs. The room illustrates how she manages to adapt the spirit of the grand stately home to smaller houses and apartments without any loss of dignity.

# HENRIETTA
# SPENCER-CHURCHILL

## MAKING AN ENTRANCE

Lady Henrietta enjoys the challenge of creating just the right ambience in
a room and has given the hallway at The Design House, Cambridge Gate
in London's Regent's Park (shown right) an imposing grandeur which
welcomes the visitor without overwhelming. She designed a geometric
pattern for the floor with specialists Attica in a combination of African slate
and limestone. By laying the pattern diagonally she creates the illusion that
the room is wider than is truly the case.

The original wood panelling below the dado was taken from the
ballroom to the hallway to add warmth, character and tradition to the hall.
Lady Henrietta uses a striking oxblood red on the walls, specialist-painted
in a distressed finish to add depth and the semblance of age, and chosen
specifically to provide a good background for the magnificent oil paintings.

Beyond the entrance, a difficult room with awkward proportions was
masterfully transformed into a glazed winter garden. The sun room, set

*Below* Visual by Miriam Topham for the
entrance hall of The Design House,
Cambridge Gate.

*Right* The entrance hall showing the view
into the winter garden, cleverly created
to add depth and light to the dark hall.

with sculptures and plants in an abundance of natural daylight, adds brightness to the more formal hall and acts as a focal point at the bottom of the main staircase. The winter garden was purposefully kept simple, with traditional Victorian-style floor tiles, and a small fountain on the wall.

## COLONIAL INSPIRATION

On the upstairs landing of The Design House, Cambridge Gate, Lady Henrietta recreates the space as a room to be used rather than as a walkway through which to pass en route to the drawing and dining rooms. The two original imposing structural steel columns in the middle of the room were used to advantage and transformed into central features (shown below). With specialist plasterers Hayles & Howe a colonial theme was established

*Above* Palm capital detail created by Hayles & Howe plasterers, with their curved ceiling behind, specialist-painted to look like an outdoor awning.

*Left* The upstairs landing at The Design House, Cambridge Gate. The space lends importance to the staircase and acts as an ante room to the adjacent drawing and dining rooms.

with palm tree plasterwork over the columns, highlighted with touches of gilt to emphasize their form while adding grandeur to the space. The addition of a curved ceiling, faux painted to give the impression of an awning, creates the illusion of the room extending beyond the interior onto a terrace or a veranda, connecting the sunlit room to the outside.

The colonial theme continues with the heavy wooden shutters and furnishings. The plaster leaves of the columns (shown far left) are humorously juxtaposed with equally monumental plants which add colourful relief to the interior. The four-seater circular chair prominently placed between the pillars emphasizes the area as a place to meet, linger and talk. The beautifully inlaid chairs and the card table provide another excuse to use the landing as a room rather than a passageway.

*Top* Detail of an 18th-century mahogany bureau situated in a restored Georgian drawing room. Lady Henrietta chose to upholster the French desk chair in an antique needlework.

*Above* Detail of a London drawing room. Lady Henrietta makes a focal point in the corner of the room with sculpture and ornamentation, mixing stripes with pattern in similar colourways.

*Right* Detail of an upper floor drawing room in a London house decorated in contemporary Regency style. The goblet-headed curtains are hung on a curved board to conceal unattractive pilasters on either side of the casement.

# HENRIETTA SPENCER-CHURCHILL

## CREATING FORMAL AND INFORMAL SETTINGS

Adapting to her client's brief and the project in hand is all-important to Lady Henrietta and sets up exciting challenges. Two dining rooms demonstrate how informality and formality can be created through colour, curtains and choice of furniture.

The striking, apple green dining room (shown below and right) has an informal, contemporary country atmosphere brought about by the rustic furniture, decorative objects and plain walls. The country-style table, chairs and oak dresser of solid rustic character are lightened by the softly painted 18th-century corner cupboard and curtains. The curtains, made from a beautiful Zoffany fabric, hang demurely on a simple wooden pole. The pole is elevated well above the window recess to take the curtains above the level of the corner cupboard, which creates a sense of balance, adds height to the window and makes more of a feature of the curtains.

The blue and white china displayed on the dresser continues the country theme and brings a touch of calm after the lively green of the walls. Likewise, the potted plant and flowers soften the look and bring in a breath of the outdoors in keeping with the overall theme.

In the formal dining room (shown below), the lack of a high ceiling or an imposing cornice is counteracted by the attention demanded by the luxurious red and gold stripe wallpaper. The curtains hang in ordered swags under the simple cornice, lending uniformity to the space. The wall sconces and candelabra add a glow that is enhanced by the warm colour scheme of the reds and golds all of which is offset by the rich mahogany furniture and fireplace. The gilt-framed mirror is hung traditionally above the fireplace and creates a sense of greater space and richness by reflecting the room. The browns of the carpet and parquet floor edging act as a foil to the vibrant colours of the rest of the room.

*Left* Detail of a country dining room in National Trust green. The dresser adds a rustic informality to the room.

*Below left* The country dining room doubles up as a hall. The green walls work well in both day and night light and complement the countryside views.

*Below* The rich, strong colours of this London dining room were chosen specifically for night use and the glow of soft candlelight.

# HENRIETTA SPENCER-CHURCHILL

COUNTRY KITCHEN

This airy country kitchen once again reveals Lady Henrietta's ability to successfully combine classical with contemporary to create a warm, cohesive room that does not pretend to be anything other than a functioning kitchen.

The cabinetwork has no adornment and uses natural cherrywood for a pared, modern feel. The high ceiling allows Lady Henrietta to take the fitted units right up to the cornice, while the glass cabinet is designed in the style of a dresser, reaching the first level of the fitted cabinets to lighten the room with the appearance of free-standing furniture. The pale stone floor is both simple and traditional, enhanced by the soft tones in the paintwork of the walls and ceiling.

Lady Henrietta keeps to the tradition of the kitchen range built into the chimney breast, adding a stone surround and internal herringbone brickwork with copper hanging pans. The 19th-century horse prints hang with a 19th-century clock high above the range, bringing authentic period pieces into play with the new, traditional-style cabinetwork.

The purpose-built hexagonal skylight over the centre island allows additional natural daylight to flood into the room, right onto the main work surface. The brass taps and porcelain double sink, reminiscent of the butler's pantry, are set in this ultimately modern central work station which is so conducive to modern-day kitchen living.

*Left* A traditional country kitchen, transformed to read as contemporary in Lady Henrietta's use of cherrywood rather than a heavier wood. The layout reflects modern kitchen living.

*Left* The almost monochromatic colour scheme and simple window treatments were chosen to avoid detracting from the dominant garden landscape.

*Right* A masculine bathroom warmed and softened by the window treatment and mahogany chest of drawers.

*Left* This narrow passage is treated as a room to provide a gentle transition from the hall to the more formal areas of this Georgian property.

*Above left* Detail of a tablescape in a Georgian drawing room.

*Above right* Silk double-tassel tie-backs, handmade to Lady Henrietta's design.

# HENRIETTA SPENCER-CHURCHILL

LADY HENRIETTA'S FIRST PRINCIPLES

- Don't assume that classic means old and historical, applied only to buildings of a certain age. Classic, as far as interiors or buildings are concerned, means timeless and trendless design, contemporary or modern but never incorporating current fads.

- Contemporary design can be classic design, but the emphasis needs to be placed on basic principles and good quality craftsmanship.

- Classic design is all about proportion and how the furniture, soft furnishings and accessories relate to the layout and overall concept of the room.

- Design should follow a coherent pattern and not include a variety of different periods and styles.

- Architectural details should be emphasized and respected and not overshadowed by unnecessary, flamboyant decoration.

- Avoid using too many eclectic architectural references as you will end up with a mélange of unco-ordinated features.

- Entrance halls should be welcoming and practical. Use hard floors in stone, tile or wood which stand up to wear and tear, and are easy to clean. If you find hard floors cold, use underfloor heating and eliminate the need for cumbersome wall-mounted radiators.

- Add visual warmth to hard floors with rugs. They will help to absorb sound and will appear more welcoming and cosy.

- Conservatories and garden rooms should be furnished with natural materials, wood, wicker or bamboo furniture and blinds. Do not be tempted to add fussy festoon blinds or curtains.

- A house should reflect the owner's personality and lifestyle. This can be achieved by incorporating personal objects, collections and paintings into the overall look.

- Do not be afraid to mix antique and modern furniture, the result will be better than many different styles of antiques and a variety of woods.

*Above* Drawing room in soft colours with beautifully detailed curtains on the French windows. The check carpet laid on the diagonal makes the room seem larger. The glass and Perspex (Plexiglas) coffee table complements the antique pieces and gives the feeling of space.

# VICTORIA WAYMOUTH

# HISTORIC
## *RESTORATION*

*Left* Library in Pimlico. The building had no period features at the outset of the project. A domed ceiling, window and fitted joinery have been added to create a sense of ordered space.

Lady Victoria Waymouth gained a solid grounding in interior architecture early on in her career by working with David Mlinaric, the high priest of decorating. This wealth of experience gave her the confidence to tackle restoration work in historic buildings, such as Goodwood in Sussex and Eastern Neston in Northamptonshire, England, with magnificent results. She employs craftspeople with all the traditional skills, and thanks to her extensive knowledge of architecture, fabrics and furniture, she manages to endow the most ordinary of rooms with the breadth and depth of the past.

Her flamboyant style, historical research and attention to detail has brought her great acclaim and recognition, and she has made her mark as an accomplished traditionalist. While always executing interiors designed to last for ever without going out of fashion, her application is still versatile, and many of her rooms speak of lightness and simplicity. Lady Victoria Waymouth's knowledge of classical architecture and her painstaking searches to track down the right antiques for a particular room enable her to create an ambience that is solid. Even on a newly-built project, she creates a feeling of timelessness.

SIMPLE GRANDEUR

Inspired by the work of Sir John Soane, the library (shown left) shows a magnificent example of Lady Victoria's traditionalism, executed without ostentation or pretension. Created in a featureless property in Pimlico, London, the plasterwork ceiling, specially made to fit the room, is arched to a central dome, articulating the substantial corner bookcases that are

# VICTORIA
# WAYMOUTH

painted to look like marquetry, an effect repeated in the window treatment and radiator cover. To avoid being oppressive she created faux block work, known as *stucco Veneziano*, below the dado rail which is studded with brass stars. The bookshelves are lightened with intermittent pieces of china and the shelves are embellished with gold and leather trim to reflect the jewel-like quality of the dado and fireplace.

In this small room the proportions have been improved to give a semblance of space and a feeling of grandeur while maintaining the ambience of a cosy, intimate sitting room. The view of a brick wall immediately outside the window is obscured by sand-blasted glass and framed by handmade traditional silk curtains edged with black and gold tassels that correspond with the all-important Empire chandelier. In houses with the right proportions she often prefers carved pelmets above the curtains rather than elaborate fabric treatments, but here she articulates the window frame with simply-dressed grandeur, working with the architecture to enhance rather than obliterate a carefully thought-out feature. The 'bones' of the room have been incorporated with conviction and purpose, and the soft furnishings work hand in hand with the new structure. Custom-made fitted carpet accentuates the shape of the room while the alcove is shaped to embrace an antique sofa; both add richness of colour with patterns that incorporate the soft golden ochre of the walls.

Lady Victoria tends to shy away from massive patterns in the most frequented rooms, knowing that busy designs have a limited time span in contrast to the timeless appeal of plains with good detailing and trimmings. In her Soanian sitting room the pattern is limited to the upholstery and carpet border with an interesting introduction of stripes to the armchairs.

## VICTORIAN SOLIDITY
Lady Victoria is the perfect designer for a collector. To her, an interior should never represent one era alone but should be a culmination of art works and furniture from all centuries, including the present day. She designs 'antique' modern pieces and light fittings that are almost indistinguishable from the originals of their time. Her 'established' library created for The Design House, Cambridge Gate, London (shown right), demonstrates how perfectly Lady Victoria is able to lend maturity to a completely new installation.

The room was surprisingly void of architectural features and character, giving Lady Victoria full scope to evoke the past. Inspired by the Victorian site, she designed a classical mahogany library of bookcases, joined by the strongly carved Doric cornice and triglyph frieze, columns that define the

*Right* The library created for The Design House, Cambridge Gate. A fitted bookcase incorporates the carved cornice to give a sense of structure and purpose to the whole room.

*Right* Detail picture showing an armchair upholstered in heavy cotton fabric that resembles tapestry and chenille, with a swing-arm light for reading. Ornaments adorn the bookcases to add informality.

bookcases and hold the room together as a complete composition. She set the scene as if preparing a canvas, giving the space substance and strength, making it ready to build on with soft furnishings. This approach gives a tremendous feeling of permanence and stability. Even the parquet floor has been specially designed and installed, darkened with polish to give an effect of age to the pattern of different woods in the tradition of *parquet de Versailles*. The rug, copied from an 18th-century design, was specially made for the room. It has all the feel, warmth and depth of colour of an antique oriental rug, and has the advantage of perfect condition and an eminently longer life span.

The chair (shown left) has also been made for the room, upholstered in tapestry and velvet, and positioned for easy reading, with a swing-arm lamp fitted to the bookcase behind. Again, Lady Victoria adds ornaments to break up the books and has painted the original door to the room with marquetry patterns to fit with the mahogany bookcases. The air conditioning with all its pipework has been brilliantly hidden away behind the casements, which

*Far left* Detail of the library fireplace at The Design House, Cambridge Gate. The club fender and miniature chairs, upholstered in a cotton fabric designed by Lady Victoria for Osborne & Little, provide an extra seating area.

*Left* Traditional Victorian curtains, in an ottoman chenille from Nina Campbell, adorn the library window. Brushed cotton from Lady Victoria's collection for Osborne & Little covers the walls to add warmth of colour and pattern.

incorporate brass mesh to resemble a radiator case. Her curtains hang from traditional Victorian poles and are beautifully articulated with trimmings and a border that enhance the subtly patterned walls that are covered in fabric from her own collection at Osborne & Little (shown above). Interestingly, Lady Victoria has chosen not to arrange the sofas around the fireplace; instead, she has most successfully created two seating areas to the right and left of the room from the doorway, divided by a circular table. The club fender and miniature chairs (shown left), covered in a rich printed cotton to resemble needlepoint, create an intimate place to sit and chat by the fireside that links the two seating areas.

## MAKING AN ENTRANCE

Even in the most opulent homes, Lady Victoria tends to keep entrance halls plain, articulating the space with beautiful stone or marble floors and giving emphasis to architectural details. More elaborate decoration is subsequently introduced within the confines of the rooms without fighting the decor of the common areas of the house. The hallway (shown right) in a house she designed in Hamilton Terrace, London, features a piece of furniture that Lady Victoria designed to hide the radiator. There is an instant formality to this space, a prelude to a serene and ordered household without fuss or clutter.

*Below* Hallway, Hamilton Terrace, London. With pale colours and a marble floor, Lady Victoria ensures the hallway does not fight with the more flamboyant rooms in the rest of the house.

# VICTORIA WAYMOUTH

### AIRY SIMPLICITY

Simplicity in a different guise is beautifully demonstrated in Lady Victoria's design for a dining room in a small Regency house in London's Hampstead. The room (shown far right) had no features whatsoever at the outset, inspiring her to create a gesso-panelled room with cornice and cupboards to give warmth and structure to the space. A chandelier and wall lights are in keeping with the formality of the panelling, and have been given emphasis against the light and airy feel of the woodwork, which has been lightened and limed.

The bedroom (shown right) in the same house is equally fresh and light in white with touches of pale blue. Timber battens have been added to give character and shape to the pitched ceiling. Set in the eaves of the house, the smallish room manages to accommodate a simple four-poster bed, economically clad with cotton voile, keeping a sense of space helped by a window treatment that doesn't encroach into the room space. The minimal *en suite* bathroom (shown below left) has a central bath panelled with rustic duck boarding that is echoed in the striped, specialist-painted walls and painted floor. With no room for clothes storage in the bedroom, the cupboards, with their sliding mirrored doors, extend the room in reflection and make it function both as a dressing room and a bathroom.

Created for informal summer evenings and everyday use, the breakfast room (shown below right) leads onto the garden. The elegant wrought-iron

*Above* A bedroom created for a Regency house in Hampstead. The simple colour palette gives a semblance of space.

*Below left* The *en suite* bathroom is minimal, but big on practicality with full-length cupboards and a central bath.

*Below* The breakfast area offers a full view of the garden.

*Right* The formal, panelled dining room was created from scratch.

# VICTORIA
# WAYMOUTH

furniture and the terracotta tiled floor create the perfect transition between indoors and outdoors, making the panelled dining room seem more formal by contrast.

## MASCULINE FORMALITY

The bedroom (shown right) in a Nash house in London's Regent's Park is formal but achieves a look that will not intimidate the male occupant. Using a mix of fabrics for the walls, window and bed dressing in colours taken from the rug, Lady Victoria adds shades of blue in the upholstery and the paintwork trims. The high ceiling gave scope for a hand-carved canopy over the bed, making the bed a focal point equal to the marble fireplace opposite (shown centre right), making the room as much a sitting room as it is a bedroom.

Stretched fabric on the walls gives a perfectly smooth finish and is edged with braid, almost as a shadow line to the simple cornice, to add interest. The ottoman at the foot of the bed, which houses a mechanically manoeuvreable television set, adds further length to the bed, giving balance to the height of the canopy and a better overall proportion.

## THE GRAND FRENCH STYLE

Lady Victoria manages to create something unique and individual for all her projects, appropriate both to the houses and to the lifestyle of the people who will live in them. The brief for an *en suite* bathroom (shown below right) was for something in the grand French style. Here, she achieves a bathroom equal to any revival bathroom created in the early 20th century in the major cities of Europe. She has created a masterful *en suite* bathroom with beautifully crafted inlaid panels of dark green and brown marble, which extends to the floor and walls. Mirrors, glass shelves, etched glass and shiny chrome basins break up the marble and add a further sparkle of glamour. The doors to the vanity unit and mirror frame are mahogany, giving a richness and warmth, enhanced by drawing room-style light fittings on the marble walls.

*Above* The bedroom of a house in Regent's Park. A canopy over the bed, rat[...] a four-poster, allows for [...] view of the windows from sitting area.

*Left* View of the sitting ar[...] the bed.

*Below* Two views of the e[...] bathroom showing the m[...] vanity unit and bath.

# VICTORIA WAYMOUTH

## PRETTY COMFORTABLE

In complete contrast to Lady Victoria's other work shown in these pages is the pretty and understated bedroom and *en suite* bathroom (shown below and right). For all their prettiness, they are not over-feminine. The low ceiling height and the constraints of a small room make it sufficient to dress the bed with a chintz floral-patterned cover with scalloped contrast-bound edging. Lace-trimmed sheer curtains in both the bedroom and bathroom hang from a simple curtain pole, enhanced by a blind in a fabric that co-ordinates with the bedcover to add colour and to shut out the light at night. The *en suite* bathroom is entered through doorless openings to the right and left of the bath so the bedroom and bathroom read as one.

## THE ARCHITECTURAL INTERIOR

In the 18th century it was considered normal practice to spend a quarter of the budget building the house and the remaining three quarters to create a complete architectural interior. In modern times, this equation is rarely adhered to, but Lady Victoria always manages to incorporate substantial architectural detailing, even if only within the principal rooms.

*Above* The *en suite* bathroom of a town house in Hamilton Terrace. Here, the central wall is flanked by a pair of door openings, making the bathroom very much part of the bedroom.

*Below* Two views of the bedroom with its pretty floral chintz and lace-trimmed voile soft furnishings.

35

*Above* A Nash House in London's Regent's Park. The 'L' shaped sofa adds informality and divides the sitting room.

*Above* This beautifully-proportioned formal drawing room is treated with traditional English style.

*Below* The furniture is placed carefully to maximize the view through the elaborately dressed French windows.

*Below* Lady Victoria has incorporated free-standing bookcases into this design to add a library feel.

*Above* A 'New Yorker' lavatory, in a
Regency house in Hampstead.

*Below* Hard floors are best for hallways.

# VICTORIA WAYMOUTH

LADY VICTORIA'S FIRST PRINCIPLES

- Before decorating, get the proportions right in the main rooms.
- Buy at least two good pieces of furniture and one quality painting for the main rooms, and if you don't have the budget for a roomful of good antiques, fill up with less important pieces.
- Buy modern, specially-commissioned carpets. They have a longer life span than antique carpets and cost a fraction of the price.
- In very large houses with large rooms, use pattern to give variety, especially in under-used rooms.
- Plain walls or damask are best for main rooms such as the master bedroom and drawing room. You are less likely to tire of them.
- If you need a large sofa in a room for extra seating, break it up with interesting cushions.
- Use low-voltage light in entrance halls and stairwells, set in the ceiling on dimmers. Avoid downlighters in the principal rooms; they give an unflattering light.
- Unless decorating an historic building, do not use picture lights over paintings. Allow pictures to be discovered without being highlighted.
- Use hard floors in the entrance halls. They are suited to wet feet, dogs and bicycles. Stair carpet can be colourful, and stair rods give a Victorian feel.

# LAVINIA DARGIE

## NEW
## *CLASSICISM*

*Left* The guest bedroom created for The Design House, Cambridge Gate.

Lavinia Dargie's creative ideas, her professionalism and enthusiasm is manifest in the simple, elegant, timeless interiors that she tailors for each individual client, reflecting her philosophy that 'the cardinal virtue of all beauty is restraint' (Elsie de Wolfe). A childhood spent in the Far East instilled in Lavinia a love of the Orient, which can often be seen to infiltrate her work in the guise of rich colours and Oriental *objets d'art,* full of character. To Lavinia, the essence of decorating is to ensure that she expresses the personal feelings, memories and needs of her clients, creating for them a harmonious home that reflects their own identity to produce an individual scheme. Lavinia loves colour but believes that it should be treated kindly and should never be allowed to overpower a room. She was influenced in her early days by David Hicks, in his use and control of lighting, his boldness in designing and working with patterned carpets and mixing old and new.

To ensure that there is a cohesive harmony of colour and function within the home, Lavinia prefers to undertake the design of an entire property. This will often include expanding the living space into the garden, and considering how the outdoor eating area will best work with the house.

### CALM SERENITY
Her guest suite for The Design House, Cambridge Gate (shown left) was situated in the basement and started as a mix of spaces divided by a brick wall, with a staircase behind that was to be removed. Working with the official architects, The Conservation Practice, and her own in-house

# LAVINIA DARGIE

consultant, Donald Ward, she has created a bedroom with *en suite* dressing room and bathroom complete with a separate kitchenette. Lavinia allows the light to filter through a simple off-white voile roller blind that blocks out the dead space in the stairwell outside, but still allows the plants on the window ledge to be enjoyed from the writing desk (shown right). Not wishing to lose any light from outside, she hangs interlined, cream wool, triple-cuff headed curtains from antiqued brass poles, with taffeta unlined curtains from the inner pole.

## TEXTURE AND COLOUR

Her use of three textures to dress the window gives a light, feminine feel to the room. It is plain yet luxurious, and pattern is introduced in the fabric-covered walls – a cotton damask from Percheron. The colour palette is serene in yellow ochres and creams; a textural mix of cottons, linens, wools and silks produces a calm ambience that feels contemporary without losing sight of tradition. The bed (shown right) is upholstered and dressed in a cotton check with a buttoned bedcover in a cream textured cotton.

A wool plaid 'Stark' carpet creates an interesting neutral background in cream and taupe, offset by the skirting painted in a deeper tone of the taupe. The furniture is chosen in light wood tones (shown below right) that harmonize with the colour scheme, sourced from The Parsons Table Company. Pictures are hung sparingly to give them emphasis, reflecting Lavinia's general uncluttered approach, and are simply grouped so as not to overwhelm the room.

## COMPLEMENTARY SITTING AREA

The comfortable sitting area (shown far right) is articulated with lively touches such as the dressing screen draped with an antique Chinese crewelwork throw and colourful, rich tapestry cushions. A sofa, tables, chair and stool are grouped to make an intimate sitting area to read the papers, watch television (a

portable TV can be set on the Perspex [Plexiglas] table from Carew Jones at the end of the bed) or sit and chat. Lavinia introduces strength of colour in the olive green and yellow ochre checked sofa fabric and softness in the pale taffeta striped upholstery of the chair and footstool. The sitting area is designed to complement the bedroom rather than contrast with it. The corner table, for instance, is a traditional element, and is set with sculpture, urn lamp and flowers (shown right).

*Above left* Detail of the guest suite window at The Design House, Cambridge Gate with curtains by Jon Rhodes and yellow vases from Andrew Martin.

*Middle left* Lamps from Yeoward South illuminate the bedside.

*Below left* A reproduction chest from The Parsons Table Company balances the table on the other side of the bed.

*Above right* A large lamp from Andrew Martin lights up the corner table in the sitting area.

*Right* The gentle curves of the damask wallcovering from Percheron act as a foil to the checked and striped upholstery on the seating.

# LAVINIA DARGIE

## DRESSING SPACE

The bedroom wall opposite the window (shown right) is punctured with symmetrically-placed side doors leading to the dressing room and bathroom to one side and the kitchenette to the other. All the woodwork is painted in two-tone off-white eggshell, apart from the dark taupe skirting which, in the teachings of John Fowler, helps to ground a room. A reproduction chest of drawers from the Parsons Table Company is placed centrally on the wall, and is traditionally set with a mirror, flanked with drawings and lit with a black and gold lamp and shade.

Lavinia uses the check fabric of the bedhead to line the dressing room walls and the shelves. A mirrored wall both gives the illusion of space and provides a dressing mirror (shown right). The check fabric is used as a pelmet heading to the yellow-gold linen curtains, making a soft enclosure rather than solid built-in cupboards for the clothes.

Halogen downlights on a dimmer provide strong light for dressing or soft mood-lighting to lead the occupant to the bathroom beyond. With little space to play with, Lavinia recruits the services of 'Gaston', the ultimate clothes hanger, and a Perspex (Plexiglas) chair from Carew Jones Associates placed in front of the mirror – all functional furnishings that achieve unencumbered space en route to the bathroom.

## BATHROOM

Her bathroom (shown right) makes perfect use of a difficult space. The bath, set back in its own wooden-fronted alcove with limestone spashback and mirror above, is treated in the same way as the curved wash-basin, the corresponding finishes creating fluid harmony. Stone-coloured walls, specialist-painted with fossil relief by Davis, Keeling and Trowbridge, the natural limestone floor with inset wooden border and the chunky wooden picture frame impart the feeling of a natural environment. Perspex (Plexiglas) is carried through from the furniture in the bedroom and dressing

*Left* A view from the bedroom through to the dressing room.

*Left* The 'Gaston' clothes hanger provides ultimate hanging space in a small room.

*Below* The bathroom from Alternative Plans makes the most of limited space.

*Top and middle* The ingenious kitchenette from Alternative Plan.

*Above* Kitchen, dining and family room are most effectively made one.

room to the Perspex and steel w.c. in the bathroom and the stainless steel basin, towel rail and taps that harmonize with the mirror. As in music, Lavinia uses certain notes and chords that recur in different guises, floating through her rooms like subtle, melodious enhancements.

## CONTEMPORARY KITCHEN

The kitchenette is no larger than a storage room, yet Lavinia manages to create a totally functional kitchen that still allows stools at the counter. A stainless steel roller cupboard conceals a kettle, toaster and provisions (shown middle left) and the sink unit, with oven, electric stovetop, dishwasher, extractor hood and microwave, are built in complete with cupboard space, drawers and a deep shelf. The walls are painted with a crackle glaze of silver and yellow ochre, a highly durable finish that gives an oriental slant. Chinese characters subtly painted into the finish mean 'good health' (shown above left). Using highly contemporary combinations of wood, polished steel and limestone, the bathroom and kitchen complement each other, and act as a foil to the more classical treatment of the bedroom.

## EXTENDED SPACE

The project for a spacious Victorian house in London required major changes. Lavinia removed one chimney breast that cut through the house, opening up the ground floor to create a flexible dining area, kitchen and family room leading onto a lovely garden. From a pair of French doors the room opens into the garden during the summer months. The open-plan kitchen is shielded from the breakfast/dining room behind folding metal screens, upholstered in gathered fabric, that divide the room in two. Formal curtains and the adaptable lighting transform the room into an elegant dining room at night for dinner parties. Leading directly onto the garden, the comfortable seating area (shown left), with a Turkoman carpet to add warmth to the terracotta floor tiles, is a place where the teenagers of the house watch television or do their homework.

Outside the French doors, Lavinia has built a deck platform for reading, eating and entertaining, extending the room beyond the confines of the house. The decking is reflected in the tongue-and-groove wooden ceiling set with downlights, giving the once-uneven ceiling a perfect finish. With wicker chairs and terracotta floor tiles, the family room becomes an extension of the garden, with the feel of a conservatory during the summer.

Lavinia never loses sight of how homes are best used and enjoyed. The room adapts to the multiple functions required by a family, as a place to gather while cooking, eating and relaxing.

# LAVINIA DARGIE

## ADULTS ONLY

The upper floor drawing room in the same house is for formal entertaining, or is a room where the adults can relax in comfort away from the television. Dark green felt on the walls adds a 'clubby' feel to the room. Rather than trying to compete with the antiques, fine prints and paintings that furnish the room, the bookcase is painted to match the walls to divert the emphasis onto the books, objects and photographs on display (shown below left).

In contrast to the dark walls, the room is lightened by a pale sand wool carpet, burgundy chairs and a comfortable sofa with bullion fringe that sits facing the fireplace. This play of light and dark colours makes the room as much a room for day as night. Red and green check curtains with swagged pelmets give the room a formal grandeur that corresponds with the antique Aubusson rug in creams and dark reds in front of the fire. The varied lamps, grouped at different heights to

the right of the fireplace (shown below right) together with the paintings in the alcoves, hung for their own intrinsic value rather than as a formal matching pair, add an eccentricity contrived to relax the room.

## FORMAL CHINTZ AND STRIPES

The drawing room in a London mansion flat (shown above right) shows Lavinia's use of a similar colour scheme to produce a completely different effect. Elaborate curtains are all the more prominent by virtue of the pale, striped papered walls. Dark green, carved pelmet cases with gold embellishments frame the swag-and-tail pelmets of floral chintz edged in dark green, making a strong statement in this otherwise understated room. The furniture is formally placed around the fire, with the dark green sofa draped with a cerise throw and tapestry cushions, giving the scheme a strength of colour. A cream carpet is broken up with small Oriental rugs that bring interest and life to the

room. Lavinia's traditional, very English approach enhances the collection of china and artworks that belong to the client, enriching the objects with cosy yet formal decoration (shown middle left).

## SERIOUS BUSINESS

The study created for the London office of the managing director of Cartier (shown below left) achieves a masculine feel, softened with feminine touches in the simple check carpet, red lampshades, antique writing table and upholstered chairs. Walls are upholstered in a Nina Campbell fabric, 'Bourbon Stripe', that is carried through to the curtains, and the flat pelmet is made up this time on the horizontal and the rolled edge is cut on the cross. The wood panelling to dado level helps to give the room strength and character.

## PERFECTION IN THE DETAIL

Lavinia has a multitude of suppliers, craftsmen and experts to hand, and she works with leading kitchen and bathroom suppliers who adapt to her design ideas, translating her vision into reality. If any of her many skills and talents are worthy of separate mention, it is her ability to interpret her clients' desires and needs and present them with a more satisfying end result than they imagined.

Her company, Dargie Lewis Designs, thrives on her own personal attention to her clients. Although she adapts to each project, her overriding signature style is always evident: sophisticated simplicity, warmth, atmosphere, quality and meticulous attention to detail.

*Opposite page* The drawing room in a Victorian house in London.

*Top and middle* The drawing room in a London mansion flat. The curtain fabric in this room is from Percheron.

*Below* The London office of the Managing Director of Cartier.

*Above* The bookcase is made of MDF and specialist-painted to match the dark green felt walls.

*Above* A small lavatory measuring only 193 x 84cm (75 x 33in) with paper-backed fabric by Ralph Lauren on the walls and a tented ceiling. One wall is mirrored to give the illusion of space.

*Below* Three different ways to dress up small windows, from left to right: Italian strung curtains; smocked heading on a pelmet; and a gathered headed pelmet with stand-up rope, all by Jon Rhodes.

*Above* Main staircase at London offices of Cartier. The wallpaper is by Van Schelle & Gurland, and the paisley design carpet from Benardout Carpets.

*Below* This dormer window treatment has a ruched fabric bar to hold back the curtain fabric.

# LAVINIA DARGIE

## LAVINIA DARGIE'S FIRST PRINCIPLES

- Get the architectural details of the room right first before thinking about any decorating.
- Rugs and cushions add instant warmth and colour, and can easily be moved from room to room – leave cushion selection until the very end.
- Fabric on the walls will give warmth and atmosphere. The fabric can easily be paper-backed and hung like wallpaper, or traditionally battened.
- If you want to have a pelmet in a room with a low ceiling, add the pelmet to the curtain itself so no light will be lost when the curtain is pulled back.
- Keep some form of continuity throughout the house. The eye should flow from one room to another without colours fighting.
- Good, innovative paint effects will age nicely, but don't get too carried away. Use them where appropriate to lift dull space.
- Make sure curtains have plenty of fullness – always err on the generous side.
- Before finalizing on fabrics, either ask for large returnable samples or even invest in a metre length.
- When the budget is tight, do not spend money on expensive fitted carpet. Use a cheap, neutral colour or matting throughout.
- Try tenting small lavatories and apply paper-backed fabric to the walls – this creates a lot of drama and character in a small, dull space. Mirror one wall to double up on the effect.
- Use processed voile roller blinds instead of net curtains for a neater, clean-cut look.
- Wooden shutters make a change from curtains, particularly in kitchens and bathrooms.
- Frame textiles in Perspex (Plexiglas) and hang as an alternative to pictures.
- Even on a strict budget, save some money for a few special antique textiles or a piece of antique furniture, it will give depth and character to a room.

# JOANNA WOOD

# TRADITION
# *TODAY*

*Left* Sitting room created for The Design House, Cambridge Gate. A contemporary look with traditional elements. The disciplined colour palette of taupe, ivory, charcoal and scarlet is inspired by the Ben Nicholson-style painting.

Joanna Wood, well-known for her almost super-human energy and charisma, has the gift of motivating and inspiring both her clients and staff alike. Her quick and professional grasp of an appropriate approach to a scheme will often echo the clients' unspoken perception of themselves. She is never closed to ideas and likes to develop the brief, not only around the building itself and the client's wishes, but also to stretch her own design capabilities. Joanna enjoys a challenge: a project for a French client involved incorporating a collection of work by Damien Hirst – dead sheep and pinned butterflies – with early 19th-century English furniture upholstered in white, and a palette of Georgian colours.

Joanna has 'the eye' and understands what will look good in whichever vernacular, a gift which cannot be taught. Getting the 'bones' right from the start is her first priority and this takes the greater part of her time. The decorative scheme falls into place as a progression once the structure and joinery for each room has been decided.

Her clients often have furniture and pictures they want to incorporate into their new scheme. Joanna will source basic pieces from her clients' collections as much as possible, but will encourage them to sell and replace items to enhance their new environment, supporting the idea that we all progress, develop and change.

19TH-CENTURY TRANSFORMATION
The brief for the sitting room in The Design House, Cambridge Gate in London's Regent's Park (shown left) came from the building itself where

# JOANNA WOOD

English Heritage wished to retain the original heavily lacquered panelling. Joanna managed to transform the room into a light, informal, welcoming space, incorporating modern paintings and contemporary furniture by David Linley, without losing respect for the 19th-century tradition of the building.

Working with specialist wood polishers Geoff Pearce, she had the panels bleached and stained to look like driftwood. The transformation is phenomenal, far from the heavy municipal effect of dark mahogany. The original plasterwork on the ceiling and above the panelling has been restored and given further focus through a painted coffered ceiling effect, using the same soft tones found in the wood panelling. Joanna hung simple beige linen curtains without pelmets to reveal the original wood carving above the windows (shown right). The curtains are supported on poles and trimmed with black and beige check lining.

The room had only one wall that did not have either windows or a fireplace. Joanna overcame this difficulty by creating a main seating area at one end of the room and a grouping of furniture in the middle with a low-back *chaise longue* that does not obscure views of the window alcove beyond. The coffee table and marquetry side tables were commissioned from David Linley Furniture, and Joanna designed a pair of elaborate, mirrored cabinets to house a television and the music system that feeds the entire house. Modern paintings, commissioned in the style of Ben Nicholson, enabled her to meet her budget and lift the room with the painterly effect of substantial artworks. She has set her own colour palette in the strong paintings, creating a room for contemporary living backed with a strong respect for tradition and the past.

*Top* These sumptuous curtains are made with one of Joanna Wood's own exclusive fabrics, 'Irish Damask' – a range of exquisitely fine handwoven Irish linen damasks.

*Above* The sitting room in its original condition, with just one light source and dark, heavily lacquered panelled walls.

*Right* The 'Gatsby' *chaise longue* in the foreground is by Lawson Wood. A mirrored cabinet, which conceals the audio equipment, was designed by Joanna Wood in baronial proportions appropriate to the room's scale.

*Below* Joanna created two main seating groups. The one here has a sofa by Lawson Wood and a lacquered coffee table by David Linley.

# JOANNA WOOD

## COLOUR PALETTE

Joanna enjoys designing rooms for clients from different cultures, and is always learning from them. Using information they provide, her designs reflect their heritage so that each project is tailor-made for the client. More and more she has found that she is creating modernist interiors for London clients and the traditional English look tempered with a continental flavour for New York and Europe.

In this elegant classical English-style sitting room, her colour palette of soft lilacs, blues and greens is lifted by the introduction of yellow, which enhances the view of the garden in the summer (shown below and right). Here she uses a simple, patterned carpet which adds complementary colour and makes the room cosy during the winter months as well as accentuating the spatial quality of the room – an Oriental rug would have totally changed the colour scheme. Not wishing to lose too much light from the large French windows, Joanna has designed simple, yet grand curtains tied back at a high level, with rope and tassel detailing in place of a pelmet.

*Above* A detail from Joanna Wood's own drawing room in her London house. This beautiful Georgian fireplace and oil painting provide the focus for the seating area as well as the entire room.

*Left* Joanna restored and decorated this wonderful 18th-century drawing room for herself. A predominantly unpatterned, yellow colour scheme gives the room a great sense of light and space. The overall effect is of calm and elegance.

## ONE-ROOM LIVING

The bedroom that Joanna designed for The British Interior Design Exhibition at Chelsea Old Town Hall, London (shown right) shows how an elaborate four-poster bed can be used even in a narrow space. The room's dimensions enabled her to incorporate a sitting area beyond the bed, set snugly around the fireplace, with a low club fender for extra seating and protection from the fire. This room had no architectural features, inspiring Joanna to make an elaborate detail of the curtain pelmets and bed corona. Her mix of patterned fabric-covered walls in the French style, the plain, detailed curtain treatment and the use of checks creates a traditional English look without too much colour to over-gild the lily. The narrow bookcase to the side of the bed takes up little space and adds a drawing room element to the bedroom as well as useful storage for books and ornaments.

## KITCHENS AND BATHROOMS

Joanna's main reception rooms will often be quite 'dressed', but she has moved towards clean lines and hard floors in kitchens and bathrooms (shown below) with no space for dirt to collect. Joanna sees bathrooms as spaces to be enjoyed and shared, and often decorates them with pictures and sculptures and a comfortable chair. She loves using stainless steel in the kitchen where appropriate, but is equally happy with traditional country kitchens in proper rural settings.

*Above* Joanna was inspired by an original 18th-century four-poster bed and had it copied for this rich bedroom. The wonderful canopied bed is the focus of the room, which is decorated in a combination of patterned fabrics in blue and ivory.

*Left* The clean lines and uncluttered design of this room typifies Joanna's approach to bathrooms.

## LIGHT AND COLOUR

Lighting is another area of Joanna's expertise. The sitting room (shown left) has no ceiling lights; the soft lilac and blue tones of the room are brought to life by table lighting alone. Thin-stemmed lamps with pleated silk shades are perfectly placed one-third of the way into the wall space above the dado level to light a pair of sculptures on wall plinths, and to break up the expanse of wall fabric. The colour scheme is vibrant and daring, with a traditional fabric pattern on the walls and strong colours in the upholstery, making a room that is a mix of the contemporary and the traditional. Bullion fringe on the sofa (shown below left) picks out the colours on the walls as well as bringing the blue and lilac upholstery colours together. The strength of colour gives life to the pale lilac fitted carpet – all is serene and comfortable without colours fighting for recognition. A note of informality comes from the lilac and white check cotton on the table. The pictures are simple and make a balanced shape above the centrally-placed sofa as a fresh alternative to a sizeable oil painting.

## ADAPT AND CHANGE

Joanna adapts to the changing world and her expertise is so broad that she can work equally brilliantly on a detailed restoration project as on a radical modern statement. Her philosophy is that the ever-changing forces of modern living require a constant re-appraisal, and she is not afraid of adapting to the 'new'.

She has enormous respect for those who have influenced the changing face of interior architecture, such as David Hicks, John Fowler and Terence Conran. Her gurus from times past are Sir John Soane, whom she finds radically modern for his time, and Robert Adam, some of whose houses she has thoroughly enjoyed decorating and restoring.

*Left* This stunning drawing room in Ennismore Gardens, London, uses fabrics by Manuel Canovas in a predominantly aubergine palette and also combines both contemporary accessories and antiques. A simple colour scheme allows Joanna to mix several patterns together, balanced by plain cream silk curtains.

*Below* This architectural grouping of pictures is flanked by lamps, tables and swags of lavender, all placed in a symmetrical formation.

*Left* Symmetry with style and function in a bedroom.

*Right* Tablescape sideboard with a formal display in front of walls covered in *toile de Jouy* fabric.

*Left The* view from a four-poster canopied bed of free-standing cupboards placed either side of the fireplace.

*Right* Joanna creates a vignette in the corner of a drawing room. Rope ties unite the pictures.

# JOANNA WOOD

## JOANNA WOOD'S FIRST PRINCIPLES

- Never place downlighters above the sofa where guests cannot avoid the harsh glare beaming down on them.
- Create both a summer and a winter scheme so that rooms can be changed easily to suit the season.
- Similarly, have a variety of bed dressing treatments so you can enjoy a change at a whim.
- Buy different styles of table-cloths, candelabra, china and glass so you can change the dining room from formal to informal to suit the occasion.
- Don't be afraid to sell pieces of furniture or paintings that you don't like.
- Avoid yellow lampshades – yellowish light gives people a jaundice-like hue.
- Before hanging pictures on your walls, set them out on the floor and experiment with layouts and spacing.

# ECLECTICISM

# TESSA KENNEDY

# COLOUR AND
# *ORNAMENT*

*Left* Bedroom, The Design House, Cambridge Gate. The small attic window is dressed with lavish curtains in a Nobilis Fontan damask. Here, the ceiling height above the cornice was created by clever use of the roof void above.

Tessa Kennedy absorbs cultural influences from all over the world, often favouring historic revivals, with an expertise that stems from her historical knowledge and meticulous attention to detail. Using specialist crafts and old-fashioned techniques, she produces finishes and furniture with highly individual results. Her work combines careful architectural planning with eclectic ornamentation, using soft furnishings and fabrics to convey an overall effect of luxury, comfort and quality. The ambience she creates represents a way of life that is synonymous with relaxation, entertaining and sumptuous living. The structural elements are all interpreted from the viewpoint of a designer and executed by Tessa's own in-house architects, and the traditional architectural enrichments originate from her aesthetic understanding of the scheme.

English-born of a Slav mother, Tessa has spent much of her adult life in the United States, giving her a truly international view of interior design. She uses objects, art works and paintings with an eclectic approach to enhance the beautiful handwoven fabrics, textured carpets and furniture that she designs specially for projects. Tessa is committed to traditional techniques, constantly commissioning dying skills such as *verre eglomisé*, marquetry, parquetry and fine plasterwork, whether for restoration work or the creation of modern classics. Building texture upon texture, such as soft velvets, damasks and tapestries against crystal, glass, wood, mosaic, scagliola and ormolu, she creates luxurious, textural compositions. Tessa is careful with her colours and tends to keep to a simple palette enriched by finishes, fabrics and art works.

# TESSA
# KENNEDY

## GRANDEUR IN THE ATTIC

For The Design House, Cambridge Gate she created, on the fourth floor, the most seductive suite of rooms to beguile any guest (shown far right, pages 60, 64 and 65). The original room had no favourable features to retain (shown right). Up in the eaves of the Victorian house, Tessa incorporated a shower room, bathroom, dressing room and bedroom to her own floor plan design. First, she eliminated the ceiling and roof joists to create a vaulted ceiling (shown far right, pages 60 and 64) to add the grandeur that her concept for the bedroom demanded, and the height required by the all-important four-poster bed with coronet.

The small attic windows have been transformed brilliantly, dressed with heavy silk brocade curtains that give the illusion that they frame much larger windows, and allow the full extent of the light to come into the room. The ceiling, specialist-painted by Mark Done above the cornice using light colours, is given height to allow the crystal chandelier to hang in the centre of the room. The ceiling height and decor, window dressing and comfortable seating combine to create a grand entertaining area on a small scale.

Tessa's design for the dressing-table inlaid with specialist-carved mirrorwork is reminiscent of the 1930s style, and the table is placed in front of the side window to benefit from the light. The walls are covered in damask by Nobilis Fontan, which is stretched to the cornice and finished with a panel of antique-looking silk velvet within the cornice to give a strong dividing line between the walls and the softly-painted ceiling. Blue glass lamps at either side of the sofa add a complete contrast of colour to the golds, creams and rich reds of the room, for an element of exotic surprise in the strict colour scheme. Heavy velvet wall hangings trimmed with silk-fringed pom-poms frame the bedroom door (shown right). The 18th-century English portrait at the far end adds a touch of sober English taste to quiet the opulent, exotic room.

*Above* Before: picture of the attic demonstrating the problems of the room; small windows, sloping walls and low ceiling height.

*Right* Tessa found the rich tartan velvet plush of the sofa in the USA. She is passionate about *passementerie* and specially designs fringes and tassels for each project, as seen on the curtains, sofas and chairs here.

# TESSA
# KENNEDY

## ROMANTIC AMBIENCE

The *lit Polonaise* with open curtain dressing and feathered coronet (shown below) is elaborate without being oppressive, offering views of the room unobscured by heavy curtaining. Striped silk is lined in off-white silk to co-ordinate with the padded bedhead, picked out in deep red silk braid to accentuate the swirling shapes. The Russian bedside cabinets belonged to Tessa's great friend Rudolf Nureyev and came from his apartment in the Dakota Building in New York. At the foot of the bed an ottoman, upholstered in contrasting fabrics, conceals a television fitted with a

motor to lift the set at the push of a button, and placed on a swivel base for viewing at either end of the room.

Tessa created an alcove for another important touch of grandeur, the substantial Russian malachite side table, setting it back to prevent any encroachment of space, and framing it with a pair of elaborate scagliola columns – an ancient Italian surface treatment using marble dust. The lighting is subtle and flattering, reflecting the reds and yellows that enhance natural skin tones. Candle wall sconces add further romance to the overall ambience. All is soft and flowing, with formality suggested by the furniture and paintings.

*Left* The truly sumptuous bedroom suite designed by Tessa Kennedy for The Design House, Cambridge Gate, with its quite magnificent *lit Polonaise*.

*Above and below right* Tessa wanted the small dressing room to look like a Russian railway carriage of the *belle epoque*. The mirrored doors of the wardrobe double the size of the room.

## EXUBERANT CULTURAL MIX

Like any stately home, the room is made up of fabrics, furniture and art works that might have been collected while travelling during the 18th century. Eastern and western European, as well as Turkish and Middle Eastern influences contribute to the scheme, for a mélange of cultural influences in the true tradition of 18th-century decoration.

The terracotta patterned fitted carpet, specially woven to Tessa's design, is covered with a handmade rug that lightens the darker colours in the furnishings. Tessa is a master at finding antiques to complement her interiors. A mirrored, glass-topped 1930s coffee table from Hollywood is flanked by a pair of English 19th-century chairs, restored and re-upholstered in dark red velvet trimmed with braids, tassels and fringes.

The bedroom, designed as part of a suite of rooms, is complemented by each area; the rooms flow in harmony of colour. A corridor leading to the bedroom has a specialist-painted door to the shower room and a curtained opening to the dressing room that leads to ornate double doors through to the bathroom. The dressing room elaborates on the Russian theme of the bedroom, and seems to be a grand railway carriage with a curtained bench seat covered in aubergine crushed silk velvet (shown above left). The alcove with the ceiling in ruched golden silk and walls in dark brown cut velvet, has the same patterned carpet that runs throughout the bedroom suite.

The wall of mirrors opposite the seating alcove conceals the wardrobes and is set with a diamond framework covered in gold leaf (shown left). A central section of the dressing area, with a domed plaster lattice-work ceiling by Troika, adopts the diamond motif of the mirrored doors. The dressing room leads on to grand marquetry-panelled double doors that are framed with mercury-gilded ormolu from Paris. They open into the bathroom and give this internal room all the importance and air of a formal salon.

## VOLUPTUOUS BATHROOM

The bathroom (shown left) is beautifully laid out, with voluptuous shapes of domed fibrous plaster arches in the ceiling, which meet at scagliola columns by Hayles & Howe that frame the alcoves for the basin and bath. A mosaic depicting a Russian-style flower arrangement is treated with the respect of an oil painting, set into its own arch above the marble-clad bath and lit with low-voltage lights. The marble floor, in terracotta and cream squares, marries seamlessly with the rich mahogany cabinetwork of the bath, column bases and vanity unit, adding to the luxurious combinations of texture.

A bronze and ormolu central chandelier fills the dome, drawing attention to the ceiling height and adding grandeur. Twinkling low-voltage lights are discreetly set into the soffits in the alcoves, and decorative silk-shaded swing-arm lamps, set into the mirror for extra lighting, add a degree of softness to the hard finishes. The Venetian mirror opens to reveal a cupboard set behind the wall above the basin, a device that Tessa created to conceal bathroom paraphernalia within the cavity of the wall (shown below left). The room has been given an architectural structure enriched by colourful finishes to create a space in harmony with the bedroom.

To complete the bedroom, Tessa created a separate shower room with toilet and basin, embellished with gold and silver-leaf flower decoration in *verre eglomisé*, a specialist 19th-century French technique. Glass panels are set into painted wooden structures that formalize the room (shown below right) and mirrors give the small room the illusion of greater size.

*Left* Vaulting the ceiling turned this small bathroom into a very grand space. Marble and wood complement each other while the magnificent mosaic panel behind the bath becomes the focal point. The mirrors add to the illusion of space.

*Below left* A close-up of the mirrored medicine cabinet, specially designed by Tessa Kennedy.

*Below right* The *eglomisé* mirrors in the shower room maximize a small space.

# TESSA
# KENNEDY

## CEILING SHAPES

A Victorian house in Old Windsor, England, needed total restoration and decorating. It was a project that evolved over some years, and the home incorporates a style that very much reflects Tessa's personal preference. The house had many marvellous architectural features at the outset, which Tessa restored to their former glory. The 'den' created for the teenagers of the household (shown right) uses the interestingly domed ceiling to add grandeur to the informal room. Painted the same colour as the walls to distract the eye from the uneven wall heights, the ceiling height is accentuated with pale blue diamond shapes that break up the expanse of soft yellow-gold. The blue on the ceiling is echoed in the central floor rug.

Furniture is set in groups around the fireplace, with a table behind the sofa for playing cards or games, and a desk for working in front of the window which is simply dressed to avoid obscuring the views onto the garden. A picture propped up on the fireplace contributes to the ambience of casual living, working and entertaining.

## GARDEN VIEWS

The substantial formal sitting room in the same house (shown far right) uses the window alcove to create separate seating for enjoying views of the garden in the summer, with a table in front that breaks up the room into separate spaces for more intimate conversation. Cream silk festoon blinds hang at the windows, and the full-length curtains are on poles, tied back to frame the bow window alcove and a panelled door that leads to the garden, creating a quiet card-playing area with parkland views (shown below far right).

Opposite the window, Tessa creates a further seating area with a white sofa set under a mirror made from a Turkish velvet tent hanging, and flanked with a pair of Victorian découpage screens (shown below near right). A coffee table in front of the sofa completes the group.

*Above* Victorian house, Old Windsor. Warm colours and antique fabrics give a cosy feel to this country den.

*Above right* The spacious drawing room with its intimate seating arrangements.

*Below left* Tessa turned Turkish tent hangings into a large mirror using antique glass.

*Below right* The window seating view of the gardens beyond.

The colours of the room are light golden and creamy, and warmth comes from cushions and armless chairs covered in earthy hues taken from the antique rug in front of the fireplace. With its elegant stucco ceiling, the large room is perfect for entertaining large numbers or, using the side seating, more intimate gatherings.

*Far left* A serene window arrangement in harmony with the country view beyond.

*Left* Close-up of the day bed in the dressing room of the suite designed for The Design House, Cambridge Gate.

*Below left* The dressing table and mirror on the right, designed by Tessa Kennedy, are available from Renwick & Clarke. Hollywood-style lights are incorporated into the mirror.

*Below* Viewed from a different angle, the whole sumptuous effect of the sitting area can be appreciated.

## TESSA KENNEDY'S FIRST PRINCIPLES

- The scale of architectural features and joinery should work with the proportions of the room. There are no rules other than that everything should relate to the space at hand.

- Work from plans at the initial stage and plot the layout of your seating arrangements and furniture on your plan. Look at architectural possibilities such as building a chimney breast, opening up fireplaces, adding a domed ceiling or putting in French windows before making decorating decisions. The structure will determine the rest of the scheme.

- An understanding of architecture, history, furniture, colour, lighting and texture will maximize the possibilities of room decoration.

- Dark rooms should be decorated with dark colours; sunny rooms with light colours. Work with what you've got, not against it.

- Use modern lighting in traditional light fittings. Lighting creates the atmosphere that enhances a room at night.

- Dress small windows to look grand, using the dead wall space behind the curtains and above the window to give the illusion of larger windows. In this way you will not sacrifice any light by having curtains hanging into the window.

- Try to achieve quality rather than quantity. Build up a room gradually if there are budget constraints. The basic architectural elements give a room the ability to evolve over time.

- Get professional advice and listen to experience; in the end this will save both time and money.

# CHRISTOPHE GOLLUT

# EUROPEAN
# *CHIC*

*Left* The spacious sitting room in an 18th-century house on Gran Canaria. An uncluttered simplicity makes for serenity and calm in this room.

Entering a room designed by Christophe Gollut is always a pleasure. The atmospheres he creates overwhelm the senses with colour, texture and mystery. Each space is tailored to the individual, in the context of the architecture of the building, its setting and prevailing climate. Christophe does not work to a formula, but has an educated instinct, an intuition for understanding the most appropriate treatment for the space at hand. He can be simple or elaborate but always gives the same meticulous attention to detail while achieving the impression that his rooms have been created through casual evolution.

A CANARY ISLAND HOME

Christophe's ability to work in the vernacular of simplicity without embellishment is no better captured than in the sitting room (shown left) of his home in Gran Canaria. Here he demonstrates his capacity to apply minimal detailing to traditional architectural elements without creating any sense of starkness. The subtle shade of pink on the walls is complemented by the quality of the Canarian light and tones harmoniously with the grey/lilac paintwork of the doors so that they actually contribute to the furnishing of the hall. Painted white, these features would go almost unnoticed and the effect would be cold and unwelcoming. The rugs are antique and blend with the softly limed dark oak strip floor. Accentuated by the unassuming architecture of the old house is a feeling of complete serenity and an almost monastic distinctness in a space where only the basic elements have been given attention, and those without elaboration. The

# CHRISTOPHE GOLLUT

hallway reflects seemingly effortless sophistication and style. Here the house is mainly used for entertaining out of doors, and the uncluttered interior makes for a welcome respite from the heat outside. The sunshine that streams into the house gives a richness of colour that, in a cold climate, might have been introduced through the use of fabrics and upholstered furniture.

Christophe is sensitive to the fact that every room has a personality of its own, even in its most derelict state. It is important to him to complement and enhance what is already there, making the most of any assets that the property may possess. The bones of his rooms are always rock solid, and the furniture almost haphazard, giving the illusion that the interiors have evolved rather than being recently commissioned. What goes on above the walls is as important as any other component. Sometimes he paints an elaborate palazzo ceiling, and sometimes he raises the eye with a stunningly simple cornice treatment.

## VIEWS OF THE PARK

His composition for The Design House drawing room in London's Regent's Park (shown right) displays both simplicity and grandeur. The room is large and well proportioned, with bow-fronted windows looking straight onto the park, which immediately suggested a theme. With such a lovely view, he wanted to bring the outside splendour into the house, making a light and airy space to enjoy as if it were an open loggia. This he accomplished by painting the ceiling with sky and greenery, allowing the original plaster beams to break up what might otherwise have been too overwhelming. Papered walls, with their haze of colour turning from green to white, add coolness in contrast to the bright sunshine that floods in through the windows during the

*Right* The upstairs drawing room, The Design House, Cambridge Gate. Park gardens outside are brought inside with cool colour and a painted ceiling.

*Left and above*
More views of the upstairs drawing room. The subtle gradation of the wall colour leads the eye upwards to the delights of the unique *trompe l'oeil* ceiling.

summer. Only one painting hangs in this room; a pair of textiles, mirrors and candle sconces are the only other wall adornments. The *parquet de Versailles* floor, made from reclaimed French oak, from Agora, London, could be mistaken as original to this 19th-century villa, and is limed to lighten the colour and show off the grain in the wood. The result adds to the serenity of the room and gives a Scandinavian flavour to the overall effect. Even the fireplace, which Christophe found in an old building that was about to be pulled down, is simple stone with no elaborate carving or monetary value, yet it introduces a substantial, down-to-earth presence.

With a different outlook and without so much natural light, Christophe would probably have placed heavy curtains over the windows. Instead he uses a simple pelmet to frame the view, and linen blinds with traditional Canarian lace trim filter the sun. Christophe has recognized the existing assets and used them to full advantage. The furniture is beautifully placed, with a central double sofa upholstered in two fabrics, and a table in front of it for lamps, flowers or a drinks tray. This device creates two seating

# CHRISTOPHE GOLLUT

areas, breaking the room up with plenty of space to move around, emphasized by the rugs that define the areas. A further, more intimate seating arrangement is set in the bay window for reading, relaxing or entertaining while enjoying the view.

Some rooms have little to recommend them and in these instances Christophe will create features, adding architectural ornament to a dull space. With his great knowledge of antiques and history, he can unearth the most stunning fireplaces to add grandeur and install chunky, oversized skirtings if the ceilings are high enough to take them. If a room has a terrible view, Christophe will shut it out and create an attractive milieu in which to live inside the home.

## A RICH GLOW BY NIGHT

Comfort is an intrinsic function of a Christophe Gollut room, whether it is to be used for the family or for entertaining on a small or large scale. Club fenders, stools and sofas are arranged in such a way that intimate groups will evolve naturally around the room without forcing people into a terrifying circle in the middle. To Christophe, the idea of moving all the furniture around for a party would signify complete failure in the successful furnishing of an ample-size room.

Christophe is a master of lighting. One would never sit down in a room that he has designed to find a spotlight shining in one's face. His lighting is always subtle, well placed and controllable on dimmer switches so that the atmosphere can be transformed at the turn of a button. In the sitting room (shown right) table lamps are used to create an intimate, cosy atmosphere complemented by the glowing fire.

## TWO ROOMS AS ONE

Another large open drawing room (shown above left page 80) has a subtle colour palette based on the colours in the Oriental rug. This room is grand without being intimidating or unwelcoming – the books left on the low stool are there to be picked up and read. Christophe often prefers stools to tables as they function both as tables and extra seating for entertaining. The fabrics work to enhance each other and add to the general play of pattern on the walls, the screen and the table-cloth, each adding excitement and interest to the room and emphasizing the furnishing. By contrast, the curtains are left plain and simple.

This room comes into its own at night when the lighting creates a new atmosphere, giving the room a comforting glow to accompany the warm, exotic decorations. A candelabra on the table, candle wall lights and the

*Right* This drawing room was created for an art dealer and connoisseur. Pale vanilla walls allow the collector a neutral space for his varied collection of images.

flicker of flames in the fireplace enhance the yellows and burnt orange in the colour palette, which can turn bright and sunny or moody and exotic, depending on the light.

Christophe has kept the opening between the two rooms so that either area can be used independently. A library table and mahogany bookcases give the smaller room a distinct function, but it remains conducive to informal entertaining. The Victorian obsession with covering chair legs is not in evidence in this room. Christophe prefers his chairs to show well-turned mahogany legs and avoids kick pleats, giving a much more open feel to the overall effect of the room.

### DIVIDING DOORS

In contrast, the rooms in Christophe's own home (shown above right) are divided by a pair of doors. This separation allows the two rooms to receive different treatments. However, when the doors are open the room beyond becomes a seductive lure by contrast. The light, murky-green room is an elegant drawing room and the dark sitting room in the foreground is for more intimate entertaining – an inner sanctum for special guests, accommodating a rich velvet-clad table for cards or for light suppers. Christophe strongly believes that rooms are to be used, and he takes care to provide furniture to allow for reading, writing, games and entertaining.

*Above left* The archway is used to create a sense of individuality for the two rooms, yet it does not divide them. Here, the same wallpaper and curtain treatments are used for both rooms.

*Above right* Christophe Gollut's own dining room leads directly into a drawing room. The striped damask *teinture murale,* combined with the rich textures and colouring used in the room, gives a dramatic 19th-century atmosphere.

He has used a pale paint finish on the dado rail, architrave and doors in the sitting room, giving, as it were, a colour introduction from one room to the next. In the sitting room we are cocooned in warmth and pattern harmonizing with stripes in a rich tapestry of texture and colour. Here, we see sumptuous decorations, oil paintings and elaborate mirrors, whereas the room beyond, by contrast, has an uplifting simplicity and lightness, with plainer watercolours and engravings adding to the softness of tones, attaching a less exotic ambience to the more formal drawing room.

## A COSY COCOON

The brief for a small sitting room with absolutely no views or natural light (shown above) was that it would be used for after-dinner entertaining and should be conducive to late-night conversation well into the early hours. Christophe has created a sense of intimacy with seating in the traditional manner around the fireplace, opened up to give warmth and the cosy flicker of flames, which he considered vital to the brief. He has used two fabrics on the walls, joined together with a wide border to create a delicate form of panelling. Fabrics are stretched over wadding to form walls that absorb sound so that conversation has no echo. The black with the blue is a daring treatment that produces an interplay of colour, set off by the red and gold in the border.

# CHRISTOPHE GOLLUT

## THE VITAL INGREDIENTS

Christophe's philosophy has changed very little over time. The introduction of dimmer switches in the early 1980s transformed his ability to adapt the lighting in a room to suit the occasion. There have also been great steps in the availability of interesting lampshades, which Christophe has exploited to the full. Often he will design his own, using varying sizes, colours and materials in one room. Christophe uses lampshades and mirrors together, sometimes turning the shade so that an image on the back is only seen via its reflection in the mirror. He brings wit, humour and a sense of fun to all his interiors, giving them a distinctive edge, which side-steps away from the stately grace of past times into the age we live in today.

# CHRISTOPHE GOLLUT

*Above and below far left* Two London sitting rooms exhibiting a mixture of European furniture and objects share a sophisticated domestic look.

*Below middle and right* Two quite different entrance halls. One is dark and Victorian with lots of mahogany and dark green wallpaper, while the other has eggshell-coloured walls and the floor and ceiling set off a collection of 18th-century botanical drawings.

## CHRISTOPHE GOLLUT'S FIRST PRINCIPLES

- Never make a dark room pale. Introduce colourful bold, strong fabrics to play off the lack of light.
- The above rule for dark rooms applies to pictures such as engravings. Dark rooms work best hung with oil paintings.
- If a room has a southerly outlook, use pale colours to reflect the light and complement the view.
- Avoid fitted carpets and install stone, parquet or matting with rugs wherever possible, even in a bedroom (very much a European attitude).
- Choose colours in their own right, not because they match something else.
- Use complementary shades of one colour to add tone and interest to a room.
- A skilful mis-match of colour will create harmony.
- If you are using dark red, do not introduce dark blue or dark green. Use black to make any of these colours sing.
- Use muted coloured fabrics that look old.
- Use dimmer switches in every room.
- Do not use brass switches; plastic is better. Switches should blend in and not become a feature.
- Use expensive fabrics sparingly so that they have more of an impact.
- Buy nice old chairs and sofas and get them restored.
- Allow the room to evolve gradually.
- Become a collector.

# ELEGANCE WITH
# *ANTIQUES*

*Left* Alidad's
award-winning
bedroom at The
Design House,
Cambridge Gate.
The imposing
William IV English
mahogany bed is
draped with an
antique pelmet
and contemporary
Italian damask.

Alidad creates interiors which seem to have evolved and developed with time. He weaves a tapestry of colour and texture that delights the eye, and then punctuates the scene with antiques and objects that lend credence to the fantasy of long-established splendour. Alidad's work is like a canvas, he starts with one colour and builds it up layer upon layer, always conscious of the overall image: the colours, patterns and textures blend and balance. Nothing jars and the overall effect is one of grandeur and comfort within an architectural framework of classical lines.

Alidad is not afraid of colour or scale; he uses boldly patterned, often luxurious fabrics such as damasks, brocades and velvets in rich colours to create a highly textured, sumptuous warmth that is elegant and supremely comfortable as well as inviting and difficult to leave. There are no set rules for Alidad and yet there is logic behind his choices: he can sense how far he can go.

## LEATHER AND VELVET OPULENCE

Alidad is a perfectionist, considering every detail, even the unseen. The proportions of a room are his first consideration and the final effect is one of matured, nonchalant elegance. In a low-ceilinged bedroom decorated for The Design House, Cambridge Gate (shown left), he has added a giant egg-and-dart plaster cornice which tricks the eye into believing that the room has the grand proportions synonymous with height. On one side of the fireplace is a long antique velvet screen, which further accentuates the illusion of a high ceiling.

# ALIDAD

Alidad has covered the walls with embossed leather inspired by a 16th-century Italian design. The art of producing patterned, dyed and gilded hide was developed in Spain. Goat and calfskins were cut into rectangular strips and painted silver, and the hides were then moistened and pressed between two wooden moulds in a type of mangle that produced a pattern in raised relief, which was then picked out with varnish or paint. In the 17th century stamped leather wall panels became the height of fashion in the stately homes of northern Europe. In this room the leather walls make a stunning textured surface on which Alidad then builds up his layers of atmospheric fabrics, furnishings and ornaments.

## HIDDEN SYMMETRY

When planning a space, Alidad hates obvious symmetry, but plays with the architecture and places objects to create equilibrium. Here he has balanced proportions with a large 17th-century Brussels tapestry from Antonio Vitulli and a tall screen. The bedroom and sitting room areas are divided with a writing table flanked by chairs, indicating the two functions of the room. 'Grand Tour' columns on the table create a visual axis and a central dividing line. Once again, Alidad demonstrates that he relishes the relationship between shapes, colours and objects to create scale and space.

The mantelpiece is made to appear larger by the height of the books and the even higher unmatched 'book-end' columns and obelisk. Humorous positioning of eccentric accessories and lamps of different shapes and sizes is a feast for the eye that softly defines the seating area, traditionally set around the fireplace. With the club fender, which is covered with a fabric from Brunschwig & Fils, Alidad has utilized the small sitting area to its best advantage to accommodate up to ten guests.

Alidad is continually pushing back walls and ceilings, creating space through the uninhibited introduction of large-scale antique furniture and dramatic patterns. Although he likes to use monumental features and large-scale paintings, here he cleverly expands the seating area even further by placing an armless sofa and tapestry chair against the walls instead of the more traditional approach of single armchairs either side of the fireplace.

## RUGS AND DRAPES

Alidad leaves the choice of rugs to the very last minute, knowing that this final element will bring the room together. He likes to use old carpets, as the natural dyes provide subtle hues. His favourites are Ziegler (Persian) rugs made at the end of the 19th century for the European market, with their distinctive, strong, palmette designs. In this room, the rug is laid on a

*Right* This remarkable leather wall covering is from Alidad Ltd. Antique furniture and paintings from Christopher Hodsoll, the mirror from McClenaghan and decorative objects from Martin Bonham-Carter furnish the room.

# ALIDAD

simple herringbone wool carpet and almost covers the entire floor surface. He prefers hard floors in dining rooms, drawing rooms and studies but understands that clients often prefer the comfort of soft and warm fitted carpet in the bedroom.

The bed is a William IV English mahogany bed from Christopher Hodsoll draped with an antique pelmet (shown below left), with hanging curtains and bed valance in modern Italian damask fabrics chosen for their quality of colour and historical references, which make them seem antique.

### LIGHT AND SHADE

As there is so much colour and texture within the room, Alidad has chosen simple slatted shutters framed with moulded pilasters, rather than curtains, which would have accentuated the width of the window and caused an imbalance. Shutters filter the natural light, adding a restful haziness and an interesting play of shadows. Curtains would have been cumbersome, heavy and too ornate.

Alidad has avoided harsh, direct lighting and used lamps that fill the room with a warm, mysterious glow accentuated by the comforting fire, which in turn is reflected off the embossed leather walls. He does not like central overhead lighting, but he sometimes uses chandeliers lit from inside to give the illusion that the real candles are generating the light.

*Below left* The bed draperies are made up of old velvet pelmets from Peta Smyth and a new fabric by Colony. Bed linen is from The Monogrammed Linen Shop.

*Below right* The wide slatted shutters from American Shutters maintain the masculine character of the room. Antique drawings from Joanna Booth.

## PLINTHS AND DOMES

Alidad's *en suite* dressing room, bathroom and shower room are exquisitely executed. Looking from the dressing room through to the bathroom frames an architectural vista of the bath with its Roman sculpture set on a marble plinth. The bathroom floor is of Jerusalem stone with a mosaic inset, and the walls are finished in textured sand with a colourwash of burnt umber to contrast with the smooth, pale floor.

A domed ceiling is lit by a strip of low-voltage lights that are hidden behind the cornice. Alidad likes to use contemporary advancements to complement tradition, often using scene-setting lighting installations to give a variety of pre-set options at the touch of a button. The doors to the dressing room are set into reveals created by the depth of the cupboards on either side. The backs of the doors are decorated in a hand-painted marquetry-pattern paper inspired by an 18th-century Italian commode. When the doors are closed, the pattern on the front of the wardrobe doors is continued right around the room.

*Above* The bathroom in The Design House, Cambridge Gate, has a stone floor and mosaic by Steve Charles. The vanity unit legs are from Alidad Ltd, and the bathroom fittings come from Sitting Pretty Bathrooms.

*Left* The dressing room showing the painted marquetry effect by Maecenas Restoration and Decoration. The hand-turned door knobs are by Ghislane Stewart Designs.

# ALIDAD

### RESTORING BURNE-JONES

Not surprisingly, Alidad's skills also extend to historic restoration. At Buscot Park in Oxfordshire, England (shown below and right), he has totally restored the Burne-Jones room in which all the panelling was designed by Sir Edward Burne-Jones in the 1890s as a framework to four of his paintings depicting the *Legend of the Briar Rose*.

The saloon, as the room is known, was in poor condition, and Alidad's task was not only to restore the walls and ceiling to their original colours and splendour but also to make new curtains and pelmets. In order for these not to look modern, garish and out of place, Alidad ensured that the British custom-coloured silk damask, also used on the walls, was hand-embroidered in France, overlaid with velvet and couched with muted gold thread. Research for the refurbishment of the Pierre-Antoine Bellangé giltwood chairs and settee led to the discovery of archival documents for the Empire silk damask upholstery, which Alidad recreated and commissioned to be woven in Lyons just as the original had been in Bellangé's day.

### AN ELEGANT COCOON FOR DINING

The Mayfair dining room (shown below) is a blend of Alidad's approach to the bedroom suite at The Design House, Cambridge Gate and his large-scale restoration work. This room was devoid of any features, but Alidad succeeded in creating a cocoon of warmth and elegance with a richly painted ceiling and walls of embossed leather hand-painted with gold leaf and pigment. Architraves and cornice were painted to simulate mahogany, echoing the dining table and chairs. The walls have no paintings or tapestries, as the decorated leather leaves no place for further adornment apart from the plain antique mirror, hung high to reflect the room. The soft candlelight illuminates the walls creating a rich golden glow.

*Left and below left* The restored saloon at Buscot Park in Oxfordshire. Wall fabric used here was specially commissioned from the Gainsborough Silk Weaving Company.

*Below* Dining room in a Mayfair apartment showing painted leather walls by Alidad Ltd.

# ALIDAD

## NIGHT AND DAY

The relationship of rooms to one another concerns Alidad greatly. If he designs an opulent, highly dressed space he will generally complement an adjoining room with a calmer version of the theme. The large drawing room (shown below and right) with three south-facing windows is painted in soft yellow and golden tones that reflect the natural light. By contrast, the study beyond faces north and is treated as a night time inner sanctum with rich reds and golds.

Originally, the two rooms were one L-shaped space, linked by a very large opening. Alidad has reduced the size of the opening (shown right) to create two very distinctive rooms, incorporating an architrave with double doors to allow separation or unity as required.

In the study (shown far right) the walls and ceiling are painted in a stencil pattern designed by Alex Davidson. The pattern even covers the cornice, creating an intimate environment in which to read or entertain friends. Exotic touches come from the textiles – the Persian carpet and the needlework chairs. The adjoining drawing room is formal and spacious. In both rooms the curtains are essentially plain with simple trimmings, as Alidad prefers to add sumptuously-coloured patterns in the furnishings, upholstery and rugs.

*Above* The reduced opening from the drawing room to the study.

*Below left and right* Views of the drawing room.

*Right* The intimate study.

# ALIDAD

RICH COLOURS AND LUXURY

This bachelor's bedroom (shown below left and right) has highly-polished, bottle-green lacquered walls with a luxurious, vibrant sheen that complements the terracotta in the marble mantelpiece. The painting immediately above the sofa is a copy of a small 18th-century watercolour, *An Audience With The Grand Vizier By Some Foreign Dignitaries,* the original of which is held in the Topkapi Palace Museum, Turkey. This specially-commissioned version, apart from being much larger than the original, amusingly incorporates a portrait of the owner in the crowd. A richly coloured textile adorns another wall, contrasting with the paintings.

Once again Alidad uses warm colours, knowing that they work well in the grey light of northern Europe:

each project he undertakes has at least one richly coloured room. The result here is reminiscent of an English clubroom that has been metamorphosed, with touches of the Orient, into the home of a well-travelled occupant of catholic tastes.

MELTING POT OF EAST AND WEST

Alidad likes rooms to look lived in and uncontrived, as though each has a history. This creates a timeless, classical look that simply evolves through experience. It could be said that although his style originates in Persia where he was born, it has travelled west to England, filtering, adapting and absorbing new influences, then settling in northern Italy, and is today reminiscent of the weathered opulence of a Venetian palazzo.

*Left and right*
The bachelor's bedroom has a wonderful 19th-century Zeigler carpet. A William IV sofa has been covered in an old Fortuny fabric.

*Above* A hallway with walls covered in felt and hung with decorative plaster reliefs from Anthony Redmile.

# ALIDAD

ALIDAD'S FIRST PRINCIPLES

- Take time to get to know the space and don't be afraid of your gut feeling.
- No matter how grand your scheme, make sure it is also functional.
- Do not hesitate to use several colours and textures – mix old and new fabrics together.
- Do not feel that you have to colour-match meticulously. It is the overall look that matters.
- Create different atmospheres in different rooms to reflect your own moods. Never match one room with the rest, but link them with subtle references.
- Where possible, try to incorporate the unexpected into your rooms.
- Be extra careful with scale and proportion. If in doubt about scale take the over-size option. Use over-sized furniture in small rooms.
- If you are working with a good interior decorator listen to his or her advice. Meeting halfway will always give the client half measure.

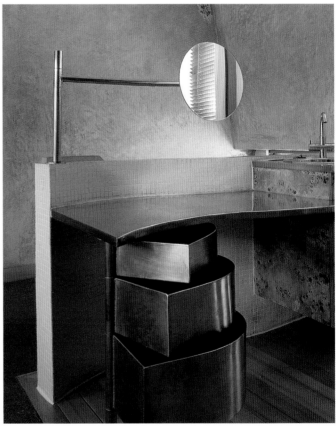

# COLOURFUL MODERNISM

# JENNY ARMIT

# DECORATIVE
## *CONTEMPORARY*

*Left* The morning room for The Design House, Cambridge Gate. Here, the floor to ceiling window dressed in voile, overlooking Regent's Park, makes a calm enclave within the larger room.

Jenny Armit is a charismatic designer, full of modern, innovative ideas which lead to exciting, original interiors. Jenny looks to the talent of contemporary artists and designers to make special pieces, sometimes to her own design, and consequently her rooms house exciting collections of 20th-century furniture, objects and artworks. Shape, colour and texture are all-important to Jenny's schemes. She creates evolving rooms full of sophisticated youthfulness and vitality, a direct reflection of her own and her clients' personalities. Her interiors exude independence and confidence and have an underlying, strong-willed femininity about them – a case of softness without the frills.

MORNING SUN, MIDNIGHT DRAMA

Situated across the hall from the master bedroom, Jenny's morning room for The Design House, Cambridge Gate (shown left), is perfectly situated to take advantage of the early morning sun and the romantic views of Regent's Park through French windows. The windows are simply dressed with sheer voile curtains and trimmed with elegant crystal tassels that reflect the light, making a cosy feminine enclave within the much larger room. The glass-topped table, engraved by Paul Clifford, is a limited-edition piece created for Jenny Armit Interiors by Villiers Brothers. It is set with simple, white, button-back 'Tallulah' dining chairs designed by Jenny.

At night the room completely alters as the silvered, interlined curtains, hung on a curtain pole in front of the bow window, draw across to give the effect of a straight wall, hiding the soft, feminine daytime curtain treatment.

# JENNY
# ARMIT

*Above* Sculptural shutters by Draks Shutters with African art that adds mood and emphasis to Jenny's design statement.

*Below* View of the morning room showing Jenny's innovative picture display, grouped to give substance to small photographic images.

## ART AND ART WORKS

Jenny's interest in art is always apparent. In this living room (shown on these pages) she includes a serious collection of 19th and 20th-century African art (shown left) set on a vellum console by Bill Amberg. She can never resist a humorous touch, and here she has introduced an element of fun in the entertaining Garouste & Bonetti limited-edition bronze figure of Atlas, filled with flowers (shown below).

Creating artworks out of as many elements as can be appropriately adapted, she gives symmetry to the asymmetrically shaped windows at either side of the room, covering each with large-slatted shutters to make sculptural, light-controlling shapes when open or closed. On the adjacent wall she displays a collection of black and white photographs in large, white synthetic frames, again made to her own design, and hung closely together to make an interesting abstract shape that reads as an art installation in itself. This fine

collection is arguably one of the most striking embellishments to the room.

The traditional morning room often suggests a way of life from times past. The cherrywood 1940s German writing desk, designed to incorporate bookshelves, allows the woman of the house to deal with household bills or write letters. The room, with its central entrance door, is naturally divided to right and left, and is furnished for dual functions, with the desk to one side and the sitting area to the other. An original Robsjohn Gibbings stool (shown below right), is set against the wall, while the 'Elipse' circular central seat, designed by Jenny Armit and Francis Vella Bonavita and covered in luxurious yellow velvet from Manuel Canovas, occupies the traditional seating space in front of the fireplace. The white upholstered 'Homage' sofa sits against the wall.

The pair of chandeliers were specially made for the room by Simon Rozenberg of Cube Lighting in cut crystal and nickel plate with linen sails lit from within. The main light source comes from jewel-like 12-volt capsule lamps set into nickel discs in the ceiling. Mirrors framed in etched wood flank the fireplace, and beneath them internally-lit tables glow at night. The walls, covered with a silver paper from Osborne & Little, add a calm, neutral yet glamorous backdrop to the light colour scheme, which is punctuated with colourful cushions (shown below right) designed by Christine van der Hurd .

The room is situated on the second floor (third storey) of a grand Victorian house, and does not enjoy the lofty proportions of the first and ground floor rooms. Jenny includes a picture rail rather than a cornice to allow the suggestion of ceiling height. The sycamore floor, designed with David Gunton, is cut in undulating ripples that resemble waves, adding a further modern element. Linen rugs from Bartholomeus Carpets are used on both sides of the room.

*Above* Robsjohn Gibbings stool. Silk cushions by Christine van der Hurd.

*Left* Central to the relaxed sitting area of the morning room is the circular seat, Elipse, designed by Jenny and Francis Vella Bonavita. Above it hangs the chandelier by Cube Lighting.

# JENNY
# ARMIT

## SILKEN DECADENCE

Traditionally, men have dressing rooms with day beds, while the women dress in the bedroom. For The Contemporary Design Show, Jenny created a woman's dressing room (shown on these pages) as a retreat from the world, in which to read, write, dress or entertain intimate friends. Here Jenny is able to let loose on a completely feminine room. Her curtains (shown above right) are two layers of sheer organza silk by Celia Birtwell, loosely draped around a curtain pole and held in place by bronze finials. The chest of drawers and free-standing wardrobe are painted and sanded to a silky smooth finish and then edged with silver leaf. Twinkling lights hang from the steel chandelier by Simon Rozenburg of Cube Lighting, with additional spot lights set into the ceiling.

*Below* The woman's dressing room: a peaceful inner sanctum.

*Above right* Curtain treatment in two layers of silk organza by Celia Birtwell.

*Middle right* Wall panelling detail with decorative corner screws.

*Below right* Detail showing mirrors by Lynn Vautrin grouped within a panel.

*Far right* Velvet *chaise longue* by Cebuan de la Rochette.

The basic colours of the room are tones of cream, a backdrop to set off the bright pink chairs by Garouste & Bonetti with their candystick legs, and the luxurious, dark turquoise, ruched velvet *chaise longue* by Cebuan de la Rochette. Utilizing the space in front of the window, Jenny suspends a double-sided mirror above the Garouste & Bonetti table, making a dressing table or a place to sit and have coffee. The screen in the corner of the room, covered in gold and navy blue striped fabric by Celia Birtwell, speaks of a theatre dressing room and adds a hint of decadence to the corner of the room (shown below).

Practically void of pictures, the smooth, matt wall panels, secured with decorative bronze corner screws, display small groups of Lynn Vautrin mirrors, making the room all the more exceptional and distinctive.

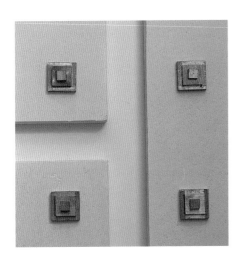

# JENNY ARMIT

### A BUDDAH IN THE PENTHOUSE

Diversity is evident in all Jenny's work. The open-plan riverside apartment with magnificent views over London (shown below) has quite low ceilings, making a large, low, empty space for Jenny to turn into living quarters for a bachelor. Positioning the furniture to divide the space, she uses a low-back wide sofa, upholstered in Manuel Canovas 'Maroquin', and makes a dining area behind it with dining chairs by Ruhlmann in curl mahogany, set around a square table. The Buddha presides over the scene, surrounded by sunlight and bamboos, giving the space the feeling of a conservatory rather than a glass box in the sky. The chandelier was specially designed to fit the space and is in keeping with the clean lines of the room.

*Below* A penthouse showing Jenny's clever use of open-plan space.

*Above right* A wine cellar of distinction, catering to every need.

*Middle right* The cabinet displays rare 1950s Italian glassware.

*Below right* Chinoiserie table with Oriental flower arrangement.

## DRINKING DEN

For The British Interior Design Exhibition at Chelsea Old Town Hall, London, Jenny created a wine cellar in which to entertain (shown left) – a glamorous men's playroom, conducive to decanting, drinking, playing cards and chatting. Void of any windows, the room is very much designed for night time living, and is lit from a recess behind the wooden cornice that shines up to light a domed ceiling.

The lace-wood veneered cabinet housing the wine is temperature controlled, includes cupboards for glasses, decanters and glass ornaments, and is lit from within, making a very definite focal point. Her colours are derived from the grape: the alcantara faux suede on the walls is the colour of white wine at the time of pressing, and the rich silk velvet from Manuel Canovas on the sofa has the sheen of red grapes as they appear just before they are picked.

Jenny's attention to detail and her ability to source appropriate pieces for each project is exceptional. The 17th-century Italian wood carving in the corner (shown middle left), for example, depicts a vine with grapes, and reinforces the thematic interior. The French limestone floor is cool and cellar-like, the hard tones of cream and grey contrasting with the warm, lace-wood skirting board.

Alcantara curtains in yellow ochre, tied back to frame the entrance door, offer a colour contrast to the walls. The Ruhlmann chair in curl mahogany set beside the cabinet resembles a throne fit for a Master of Wine. All in all, Jenny's mix of textures and complementary colours is both harmonious and seductive.

Jenny is never one hundred percent conventional, particularly in her picture hanging. She likes art works to breathe without surrounding clutter. The 1920s Chinese cinnabar shelving unit (shown left) has a pair of small pictures above it and a candle sconce by André Dubreuil that adds moody light and a balance to the pictures. Without the sconce, the pictures would look lost on the large wall.

# JENNY ARMIT

Jenny is as at home with a blank canvas as she is with grand houses with elaborate architectural detailing. A London house (shown below) illustrates how she transforms traditional space into a contemporary statement. Painting the walls white, in keeping with the Georgian fireplace, immediately gives a contemporary backdrop to her colourful articulation of fabrics and modern furniture.

The sofa design, with its tight, smooth upholstery, has an elegance of line that conforms to 18th-century tradition. The tangerine raw silk curtains with pleated pelmets hang down to the floor, accentuating the ceiling height and framing the window behind the sofa, which becomes part of the wall with its simple beige silk blind. The beautiful flower vase in blue and white glass demands tall-stemmed flowers that fill the space between the curtains and the gilded mirror and commune with the ethnic wood carvings set upon the radiator-cover shelf behind the sofa.

The unconventional double-height wooden circular side table is a Finnish piece and the wood and steel stool by Philippe Starck doubles as a coffee or drinks tray. A simple, large green glass bowl placed in front of the fire adds a touch of colour that vibrates with the orange tones of the curtains.

The juxtaposition of so many surfaces adds informality to the grandeur of the space, making an ideal environment for relaxed living with friends. The neutral colour of the plain carpet holds the whole scheme together.

*Below* Traditional drawing room with Lutyens chair, Philippe Starck stool and double-tier 1950s table.

## FOLLOWING A CURVE

Landings are as important to Jenny as any other part of a house that she designs, and are given equal consideration to achieve a unified design statement. The top landing of a 19th-century house in Notting Hill, London (shown below left), has been developed as an extension to the bedroom, displaying African art works on an undulating jade shelf, lit from the steel-framed skylight in the ceiling.

Curving the wall turns the passage into an intimate art display to be enjoyed coming up the staircase. The steel skirting reflects shafts of light that glow when the sun shines, lighting up the fish-skin panel above.

## HARD-EDGED COMFORT

The bathroom in the same house (shown below right) was a long, narrow room at the outset. Jenny fitted the bath under the window and brought the wall forward to incorporate a separate steam shower room with a glass door. The heated radiator bars are conveniently positioned to service both bath and shower while adding an industrial, hard edge to the scheme, in contrast to the warm mahogany of the double vanity basin, and the slatted Venetian blind covering the window above the bath. A shade of apple green, well known as a calming colour, induces relaxation during bath time.

*Below The* hallway with its curved wall, art display and fish-skin panel leading to the bedroom.

*Below* Bathroom, Notting Hill. The stainless steel heated radiator bars give a sculptural element to the scheme.

*Above* The playroom in a west London house, showing the view through to the *en suite* kitchen.

*Above* Playroom with children's work table, chairs and library, viewed from the kitchen.

*Below* London loft development with foreground chair and stool designed by Christopher Nevile.

JENNY ARMIT'S FIRST PRINCIPLES

- Use space to full advantage. Bring light in if a skylight or French windows are possible.
- An interesting contrast of colours is far better than a mediocre or 'off' match.
- Always employ a lighting consultant. Bad lighting can ruin a room.
- Use light to change the atmosphere from one mood to another.
- Commission specialist pieces with the advice of someone who has an eye for collecting.
- Collect works of art from today's artists, whether painters, sculptors or furniture makers. Collectable pieces will add substance to a good interior.
- Add humorous touches and don't be afraid of your own individuality.
- Create an atmosphere that is conducive to the usage of the room.
- Be brave!

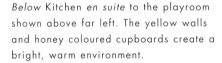

*Below* Kitchen *en suite* to the playroom shown above far left. The yellow walls and honey coloured cupboards create a bright, warm environment.

# PHILIP HOOPER

# THE ORNAMENT
## *OF SPACE*

*Left* The Design House, Cambridge Gate. The marble bathroom in two contrasting materials, Estremoz from Portugal and yellow Brecchia from France. The masonry work was done by Stoneworks. Hand-embroidered towels from Renwick & Clarke hang on the heated towel rail.

Luxury, modesty with flamboyance, order and restraint sum up the paradoxical and instinctive design philosophy of Philip Hooper, a designer who mixes traditional ideas with new technology and achieves some spectacular results. Philip is meticulous in every aspect of the design process, from the configuration of rooms and their proportions to the final ambience created by a mix of fabrics and furnishings, often made to his own designs. He builds his creative ideas at the outset, producing scaled floor plans and elevations so he can get a feel for the architectural elements. From these beginnings he evolves a concise, overall picture of the design concept, presenting the client with full drawings and perspectives, which he usually draws up himself. Nothing is finally decided until a fully finished picture of the total result has been established.

Philip has an extensive academic knowledge of architecture and period detailing, which allows him to superimpose classic ideals and translate them into modern idioms, using modern materials to manipulate the traditional style that is appropriate to the period of the building. His company, Philip Hooper Design Associates, is a partnership with the architectural practice of Jones Lambell. Every project they undertake is very much a team effort, and they are in demand all over the world, particularly in the United States.

AN INNER SANCTUM
The bedroom suite for The Design House, Cambridge Gate, began with a scale drawing of two rooms in which to accommodate a bedroom,

# PHILIP HOOPER

bathroom, shower room and dressing area by configuring the walls to suit. The bathroom (shown below, and page 110) shows how the team creates rooms with classical geometry, with a central space for the bath and vanity basin, which are symmetrically placed at either end. Separate rooms are created for the toilet and bidet and for the shower that drains directly into the marble floor.

The rooms are classically detailed, embellished with etched glass edged in stainless steel, and mirrored doors that add contemporary technology and style. Philip uses doors to full advantage, mirrored in the bathroom to create the illusion of greater space, and symmetrically placed to make a myriad exits and entrances in reflection. The colourful frieze picked out with paint in the cornice, and the inlaid marble floor give strength to the pale colours of the room and define the space. By contrast, the soft colours with the sheen of polished marble announce a spiritual inner sanctum of cleanliness. Privacy is accentuated by a lobby of veneered cupboards that divides the bedroom from the bathroom, making the bathroom a secret room, unseen even when the jib door in the bedroom is left open. When closed, the door is concealed, decorated with skirting and fabric to match the bedroom walls, sealing off the jewel-like room that is hidden beyond.

*Above* The extra-deep cast-iron and enamel double-ended bath is centred in a marble-lined niche.

*Left* The vanity unit has chrome legs and frames made to Philip's design by I M Products, who are also responsible for the doors and mirror frames. The right-hand mirror houses a flat-screen television set behind an etched, glass square, supplied by Sound Ideas.

## TEXTURE, WARMTH AND COMFORT

The bedroom (shown below) is as soft and comfortable as the bathroom is clean and hard-edged. The room has been textured with fabric and warmth of colour that derives from the colour scheme in the bathroom. Philip uses a strong plaster cornice, reflected in the mahogany canopy of the four-poster bed. The crisp linen 'cherub' fabric, specially designed by Philip with Brian Lawrence to dress the bed and windows, is lined in beige cotton and adds a subtle femininity that balances the formality of the furniture layout and the masculine colours. The generous curtains are held back low down while a matching blind is lowered across the window.

The walls are covered in a subtle shade of caramel brushed cotton, making an undisturbed backdrop against which to display a collection of modern paintings, sparingly hung to emphasize their importance. Much of the furniture is antique, but it includes a pair of Philip's sycamore bedside chests with touch-catch drawers veneered in a combination of woods. This successful mix of antique with modern pieces might almost go unobserved, due to his careful use of traditional materials and furniture-making techniques. He adheres to colours that meld in a harmonious dance, elevated by hints of heavy golden silks and rich burgundy velvets in contrast to the cottons and linens of the main fabrics.

*Right* The bed, commodes and tall cupboards were all made by Archer & Smith to Philip's design. The ruby glass lamps and other table lights are all by Charles Edwards.

# PHILIP
# HOOPER

## ARTFUL DECEPTION

No two projects that Philip designs will ever be the same. They will, however, all have a common understanding of ergonomics, comfort and luxury, with a style that hangs on firm architectural foundations. The Victorian mansion apartment designed for an American client with an enthusiasm for the 1930s (shown on these pages) required a total re-organisation of space. From the initial plans, Philip made a series of interconnecting rooms *enfilade*, using salvaged 1930s glazed doors that read as original features of the apartment, adding light and giving a general feeling of openness to all the rooms. Set directly opposite each other, the doors, when partially opened, give the artful impression that the rooms continue beyond the last room, an illusion that is shattered when the double doors are opened wide to make a spectacular entertaining space. A group of contemporary prints by Sir Terry Frost are hung in the dining room to harmonize with the symmetrical glass panels of the doors.

*Below* Teak doors from London Architectural Salvage (LASSCO) are repeated throughout the apartment.

*Top* Betty Joel armchairs are upholstered in antique linen suiting fabric. A 1940s Italian low table is from Gallery 25.

*Above* Throughout the front of the apartment the windows are hung with natural Majorcan linen curtains.

The ample ceiling height gave Philip the opportunity to use a substantial, oversized skirting throughout the apartment, painted in green taupe to suggest age and to complement the original oak floor, which he had sanded, stained and re-finished. Some of the fitted joinery has been specifically sourced from salvage merchants, contributing to the illusion that the architectural elements are original to the building, rather than recently added.

## STRUCTURE AND DETAIL

With panels of bevelled mirror over the chimney breast, the drawing room (shown left) is lightened and given the appearance of increased width. All is simplicity, and the architectural elements contribute to the visual decoration, including the wenge wood and slate fireplace, which was designed by Philip to give further substance to the overall scheme and forms a pair with one in the dining room. The detail is all in the structure, with plain, white-upholstered furniture acting as accessories, set upon a discreet two-tone dhurrie that the client brought back from a trip to India. The painted American cabinet (shown above left), brought to England from the client's collection in the United States, and the Art Deco pieces found by Philip, give the room a collector's touch.

Philip uses the narrowness of the room to advantage, placing the Art Deco chairs by Betty Joel – an important female designer working in that period – at close quarters for an intimate, rather than formal, drawing room. The bow window is simply dressed in cream linen, specially woven in Majorca and hung on forged steel poles (shown left) for an unpretentious finish that complements the room. The windows throughout the front of the apartment are hung in this way.

Philip's subtle use of pale neutral colours for the furnishings contrasts well with the dark oak floor, and warmth exudes from the burnished green-gold dust on the walls, painted onto a caramel-coloured ground, that makes the walls glow in varying colour tones to echo the reddish hues of the woodwork. Harmony of colour within a room is paramount, and the beautiful colours of the 19th-century American cabinet, painted with naive Dutch country scenes, are unobtrusively reflected in the colour scheme.

The relationship of rooms to one another is a vital component in Philip's overall concept. Using a strong shade of green in the kitchen, glimpsed when the doors are left open, he introduces the eye to glowing colours beyond the drawing room. Looking another way into the dining room, the square, wooden-framed upholstered dining chairs echo the wooden-edged Betty Joel armchairs.

# PHILIP HOOPER

## MAHOGANY AND STAINLESS STEEL

The kitchen (shown below) has Edwardian notes due to Philip's use of salvaged solid mahogany doors and a dark counter of exotic hardwood. The mahogany mixed with the organic forest green and high-tech stainless steel components creates a design that unites early and late 20th-century references. Windows with glazing bars that reflect the look of the 1930s doors are left uncurtained, keeping to the theme of clean lines without unnecessary embellishment; this is, after all, a working kitchen for a serious cook. The terracotta tiles are set square behind the range top and are laid on the diagonal on the floor, using geometric considerations to enhance the space. Philip adds all the necessary practical touches, incorporating a magnetic knife rack in the tiled wall beneath the steel extractor hood and concealing a refuse drawer beneath the granite chopping board.

In the breakfast area built around an original table and chairs designed by Arne Jacobsen in the 1950s, Philip includes a bench seat for economy of space, upholstered with fabric designed in Japan by Nuno (shown below right). Painted duck boarding, taken up to a high dado level and defined by a painted beading in wenge, visually confines the eating area to an alcove within the kitchen. The whole room is a fine example of effective visually pleasing and practical design.

*Above* Original Arne Jacobsen chairs and table in birch are juxtaposed with a contemporary Japanese textile found by Philip on a trip to Tokyo.

*Left* The kitchen units are painted in a flat blue-green highly favoured by Arts and Crafts designers.

## A BLUE-GREEN COCOON

The *en suite* bedroom (shown right) is flooded with light during the day, and becomes a cocoon by night. By designing the bed as a unit that incorporates a fitted bookcase immediately under the pair of windows, Philip creates a place to lounge on as a day bed, and for reading, day-dreaming and lying back to consider the stars at night. When the slatted Venetian blinds are down, the windows turn into minimalist art works or tall-backed headboards, an illusion that changes the ambience of the room completely.

Bedside lights fitted into the wall behind the bed for night-time reading also light the display of antique American andirons on the window sill. The dark blue-green room transforms into a study by day. An antique bureau and dark wood furniture are lightened by the neutral linens, biscuit-coloured raw silk and sea-grass matting. The owner's collection of prints is hung with conformity throughout the apartment, a theme that brings a rapport to all the rooms.

The compact bathroom (shown below right) is structurally squared-off by the bath, which has been made into a bathing retreat complete with a heated towel rail set on granite ceramic tiles. The large mirror above the basin doubles the space in appearance and is lit with halogen ceiling lights on dimmer switches. Granite, streaked with tones of terracotta, green and grey, covers the concealed cistern below the mirror and flanks the bath to pull the room together and echo the colours used elsewhere in the apartment. With no window to dress, the 19th-century French linen shower curtain adds softness to the hard finishes.

*Above right* The study-bedroom works equally well by day and night.

*Right* The bathroom is lined in granite-style tiles from Domus.

# PHILIP
# HOOPER

## A TURQUOISE ACCENT

Philip's diversity and ability to adapt to each particular project is evident in the apartment above former stables in a Belgravia mews (shown on these pages). With no special features to be restored or retained, Philip was able to open up the poky rooms of the past to create a contemporary living space that brings all the rooms together. Oak floorboarding runs throughout the apartment, and a sisal rug bound in leather adds a touch of comfort to the sitting room while defining the space in place of walls.

Colours are carefully chosen to avoid any possible blandness: a soft living area opens into a brightly coloured kitchen that accessorizes the living area like a well-lit cobalt glass bowl. The kitchen, with its glazed ceiling, is flooded with light during the day and lit at night with downlighters on dimmers, allowing a constant focus on the turquoise of the fitted cupboards that is all-important to enlivening the duller tones of the through rooms. By introducing turquoise into the sofa cushions in the sitting room and the table cloth in the dining area (shown left), Philip provides stepping stones of colour that lead the intrigued eye through the space to the turquoise kitchen beyond. The walls, painted in yellow ochre and hand-papered with over a thousand rectangles of white parchment, lead through to plain walls in the kitchen painted in the same yellow ochre colour.

*Above left* Custom-designed sofa from Philip Hooper Design Associates covered in silk/linen stripe from C & G Partnership. All the furniture is French and Italian of the mid-20th-century from Gallery 25.

*Left* The dining table, set with porcelain in varying tones of caramel, brown and gold. A built-in banquette was made by Archer & Smith, and the chromed lights are from Besselink & Jones.

Each element has a carefully thought-out association with another – even the horizontal slats of the Venetian blind (shown right) provide a juxtaposition to the vertical stripes in the curtain fabric. Geometrically patterned cushions and the mosaic surround to the fireplaces (shown below right) pick up the vital colours of the scheme. The harmonious palette of white, green, brown, beige, yellow ochre, grey and blue, communes with the naive painting of an Indian elephant, which in itself has a further relationship with the inlaid mother-of-pearl Indian-style tables that flank the fireplace. To ensure the flow of design communication between the open-plan rooms, Philip uses the striped handwoven Italian silk and linen fabric to cover the bench seat fitted to the wall along one side of the square dining table. The table, placed off-centre to accommodate the bench, gives room to pass to and from the kitchen and lets the view flow through from the sitting room. For minimal visual complication, the André Arbus-style dining chairs are covered in a felt that complements the faux suede of the armchairs in the sitting room.

## THE BARE ESSENTIALS OF STYLE

All Philip's work is consistent with a painstaking ability to produce what is most appropriate for the project at hand. Nothing is ever overdone; his rooms are usually edited down to the basic essentials and void of unnecessary ostentation and contrivance.

*Above right* The curtain fabric, from C & G Partnership, is hand-loomed in Florence, and the floor lamp in bronze is from William Yeoward.

*Right* The sitting room pivots around a custom-designed ottoman from Philip Hooper Design Associates, upholstered in herringbone-stamped suede.

# PHILIP
# HOOPER

*Above right* 1970s Snoopy lights by Flow sit on a Gordon Russel-style sideboard. The pictures behind are textile designs by Sonia Delauny.

*Below right* A 19th-century French day bed is covered in blue linen cushions from Bernie de la Cuona.

*Below* A two-tone veneered dining table by Betty Joel is surrounded by chairs also to her design. The brown upholstery fabric is from John Stefanidis.

# PHILIP HOOPER

## PHILIP HOOPER'S FIRST PRINCIPLES

- Get the architraves and skirtings right. Don't be afraid of removing incorrect ones and replacing them to have correct proportions in the room.

- Don't use skinny, mean profiles in a traditional room setting.

- Take time choosing your lampshades. Avoid novelty shapes – instead choose simple, chic coolie or slightly tapered shapes. Choose varied colours and line them with contrasting fabrics.

- The proportion of a lampshade base is vital. Bases should vary from porcelain or china to bronze or wood. A selection of lamps will add interest and informality to the overall result.

- Curtains should always be drawn out to scale before they are made up. There are specific rules for pelmet size in relation to the drop. Grand curtains should be made up as a 'toile' first, i.e. in canvas or calico, as with couture dresses.

- There is always a solution to dressing the most awkward of windows, even if it means having no curtains at all. Always use a heading that takes the shape of the window into account.

- Build joinery into a room whilst respecting the period of architecture that is already there, to keep the spirit of the building consistent.

- Don't be afraid to use large pieces of furniture. Strong architectural pieces will give a rhythm to a room, often where none previously exists.

- Do not take shortcuts to save on your overall budget. It is much better to wait until you can afford to do it all properly.

- If possible, live in a space before you start altering it – maybe even paint it white. You will then discover exactly how to re-organize the rooms to suit your particular lifestyle.

# CHARLES RUTHERFOORD

# COLOUR
# *AND FORM*

*Left* Victorian apartment, south London. An *enfilade* from bedroom hall to library hall, has mirrored doors at a high level reflecting the lit ceiling to give a complex layering of spaces. The drawing room at the end of the view has a rushwork and steel sofa by Charles Rutherfoord.

With his expert eye, Charles Rutherfoord is able to create a completely contemporary setting, even in the most traditional of homes. By always looking at the architectural possibilities of each project, he ensures that the 'bones' of the space set off the contemporary design for which he is so well known. With a leaning towards the minimal, he creates an atmosphere of calm through the clever use of colour, form and texture.

His rooms are never cluttered, and they often give focus to major art collections. Charles' interiors are understated and serene, adapting to both formal and simple living. His designs have a sophisticated youthfulness and vitality that accommodate the demands of a frantic modern life. Good storage is provided everywhere so that even bills, newspapers and the general clutter of day to day living can be swept unseen into ordered and controlled compartments.

SMALL SPACES MADE LARGE

Charles' use of space is phenomenal. He creates rooms within rooms, making transformable spaces without unnecessary complications. A fine example of this is his design for a Victorian apartment in a south London detached house. Charles completely re-modelled the hallway (shown left), stripping out the limiting configuration of rooms to create a far more functional space. Keeping the cornice in the main room, he has reduced the size of the landing to create a small library, and cut a hatch opposite the bookcases to form a deep, mirrored desk area at waist level with closing panels on both sides.

# CHARLES RUTHERFOORD

Above the bookcases, he uses mirror again to expand the space, reflecting the slatted, lit ceiling of sand-blasted glass and beech, a tribute to turn-of-the-century Viennese architect Adolf Loos. Glass panels slide over the bookcase, which are flogged with wide brush strokes in white emulsion and purple varnish. Overdoors, a much loved 18th-century feature, are re-interpreted by Charles, using photographs by Judy Goldhill set behind glass at either side to form part of the room's structure. Charles designs most of his furniture, such as the steel-framed sofa with woven rush that can be glimpsed through the doorway in the sitting room beyond. The doorway ingeniously hides double doors within its reveal.

## LARGE SPACES MADE SCULPTURAL

In contrast, the kitchen (shown right) that Charles designed for The Design House, Cambridge Gate, makes stunning use of an enormous space to accommodate kitchen, breakfast room and pantry. Here, he architecturally divides the area, using columns with cupboards at their lower level, visually linking the kitchen to the breakfast room and opening both areas to the courtyard outside via French doors. The sculptural ceiling conceals pipework and light fittings, and incorporates a graceful extractor hood that emerges from the undulating curves of the ceiling. In the breakfast room he commissioned ceramic sculptor Margaret O'Rourke to make a sculptured chandelier to hang above the table of his own design (shown right).

Charles uses finishes and textures in abundance. They are carefully chosen to enhance each other in tones of reds, browns, golds and greys, and in a mix of hard and soft finishes, both natural and manufactured. A stainless steel flower arranging sink is set at the far end of the kitchen area, around which he has created a sitting area with sheer curtains lit from the ceiling to bring out their silken quality. To the right of the sink a waved screen veneered in charcoal-stained timber set in squares provides visual relief from the walls of storage.

*Right* The Design House, Cambridge Gate. The curvaceous ceiling with integrated plastered extraction hood conceals much of the lighting and adds interest to an often-neglected element of the room.

*Below* Metallic finishes in the kitchen and breakfast room add richness and warmth. The sofa, by Charles Rutherfoord, is in copper-finished fibreglass, the columns are covered in patinated copper Japanese paper.

# CHARLES
# RUTHERFOORD

## DUAL-PURPOSE SPACE

The bedroom with bathroom (shown left) was created for a bachelor in London's Notting Hill. Built in the 1970s, and with no original features to worry about, the house contained a number of poky rooms. To expand the space, Charles knocked through two bedrooms and a lobby to create a single bedroom with bath, basin (shown below) and shower.

The pole with attached mirror punctuates the separate functions of the unified space. A basin plinth of cast concrete was moulded in a three-quarter circle in a rough wooden frame to take on the indentations of the wood grain of the Douglas fir. The remaining quarter circle, set underneath the stainless steel sink, provides access to the plumbing and storage. A shower tray extends around the basin unit to contain the water from the open shower, and has a white, textured non-slip finish. From the doorway of the room, a bowed screen in polished stainless steel shields the bath and reflects the light from the window which is positioned immediately opposite.

There are no applied finishes in the room, the blue back wall is treated with polished, pigmented plaster. The use of natural materials extends to the ceiling, which is rendered in a natural grey plaster. Charles creates a decorative post-and-beam detail around the bed, with a glass panel cut into the thickness of the floor above allowing shafts of sunlight to filter through from the skylight in the roof. Each element is set at an angle, independent of the grid of the rectangular space. The panel of display boxes behind the bed gives a sculptural effect, and the boxes are angled with niches of different depths to add length to the room and create a wide-angled architectural space. The bed, made from cast concrete, is cantilevered with a recessed base covered in the same granite tiles used for the floor.

*Left* The main body of the floor plan is used to make a single large space for the bedroom and bath, shower and basin. The back wall is in a special polished plaster finish developed by Charles Rutherfoord.

*Right* Detail of the basin top in Perspex (Plexiglas) flogged with white emulsion and colour varnished on the underside.

# CHARLES RUTHERFOORD

## MODERN TAKE ON THE 19TH CENTURY

Charles' library for a terraced house in London's South Kensington, (shown far right) preserves all the original 19th-century features. The house was in disrepair at the outset of the project, with badly damaged cornices. Charles hides the cornice behind bulkheads with inset lights to throw light across the ceiling. He has restored the shutters on the windows and the original oak floor, lightening the wood to give the traditional parquet a modern, fresh and contemporary feel.

The books on their orange laminate adjustable shelves can be concealed by galvanized steel sliding doors re-finished in fake antelope framed in blue lacquer, giving the room an instant change of face. Charles designed the centre table, found a copy of a Frank Lloyd Wright chair and placed a 17th-century Chinese stool in the corner.

The steel and pine staircase (shown below right) is enamelled to match the blue of the library doors. Underneath the staircase is a flower arranging sink in stainless steel and granite, which can be seen from the kitchen through a double-sided cabinet with sliding doors (shown below).

*Below left* Flower arranging sink with flame-textured granite top cantilevered off-centre on a stainless steel column.

*Below right* Detail of steel and paranha pine staircase; cantilevered treads with open risers give a view through to the flower arranging sink under the stairs.

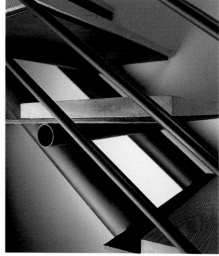

It is not unusual for Charles to work with a particular client for many years, adapting their living space to accommodate their changing needs. After completing the library, Charles was invited back to the house to build a drawing room extension (shown below). The classical lines of the monumental doorway, with viewing columns that give a glimmer of the new room beyond, reads as an architectural element as well as a sculptural statement. The opening, in total harmony with the two rooms, has no need of doors. A similar portal at the opposite end leads to the study, completing this visually stunning space.

The fireplace (shown left), void of a mantelpiece, is a statement of total simplicity. It is, in fact, a monumental, free-standing piece of sculpture, the wall having been brought forward of the chimney breast in order to gain space behind the back-lit display niche. The fireplace, which is used for wood and coal, is thus given extra depth, a deep black hole that juxtaposes the smaller, light-filled square above. The walls are polished plaster with touches of bronze, and are finished not with skirting but with a simple aluminium channel at the base.

*Below left* Detail of the chimney piece in bronze-polished plaster. The chair is mid-18th-century American.

*Below right* The library after the addition of a drawing room seen through a portal with slots of light to each side.

# CHARLES RUTHERFOORD

## ILLUSIONS WITH COLOUR

Charles often picks out one wall in a different colour. The all-white dining room (shown below left) has one orange polished plaster wall. By designing a two-way pivoting door, he links the dining room to the kitchen and creates the illusion that the coloured wall has been dropped into a bigger space, making the room seem much larger. A thin channel at the top of the walls in place of a cornice gives the room the impression of greater height.

## PERFECT SYMMETRY

The bedroom (shown below right) smacks of traditionalism with a modernist twist. Here the furniture is arranged with perfect traditional symmetry, and a fireplace was sourced to fit within the period of the 1840s house and the 1770s English chairs. Yet there is much that is unexpected in this particular composition. No painting hangs above the fireplace and the industrial radiators act as modern sculptures in the room. Charles introduces lighting that shines up at the pictures through the floor, using white walls with ivory and grey carpet to highlight the furniture and pictures as art works.

## VIEWING PLATFORM

The breakfast room (shown below left, opposite) looks out onto the garden through a window placed high in the wall. To make the most of the view, Charles has placed a cantilevered wooden floor on top of Japanese unglazed mosaic which continues throughout the basement of the house. In channels underneath the platform, he conceals strip lighting so the floor seems to float.

Charles designed the orange enamelled steel benches that cantilever off the wall to create extra seating with style. His use of colour and texture produces graduated tones of richness and simplicity, the limed oak table top harmonizing with the natural weave of the seats.

## METAL, WOOD AND MOSAIC

For a project in Chelsea, Charles added a low architectural wall in unglazed ceramic mosaic to separate the staircase from the bath area (shown below right, opposite). Pivoting stainless steel drawers sit underneath a copper-topped dressing table that is fixed to the wall. The inset basin is of burr poplar and the stainless steel column supports a rotating mirror.

*Above* Bedroom with 1840s chimneypiece flanked by radiators.
*Left* Dining room with door set into polished plaster wall.

*Above* Dining room showing a new chimney piece and laminated touch-catch cupboard units.

## A DUAL-PURPOSE DINING ROOM

The dining room (shown left) in a Victorian house was masterfully transformed from a 1970s kitchen into a contemporary room. Both the stovetop and hood were originally located in the chimney breast, which Charles filled to create a fireplace. Flush laminated doors with touch-catches give a continuous plane to the wall while accommodating deep storage cupboards. Soft and gentle tones of lilac, pale green and stone contrast with the painting by Martin Fuller above the fire. The floor of 17th-century French limestone, adds a rustic element to the otherwise modern finishes in the room. Sliding laminated doors cover the wall opposite the fireplace, hiding music, television, books, videos and paperwork. The room is multifunctional, adapting to both formal and informal entertaining while doubling up as a family room that is easy to tidy up.

## COMFORT AND HARMONY

Chaos has no place in Charles' installations. All is order, comfort and harmony, with pleasing colour and textural combinations that infuse his spaces with warmth and luxury. There is no fuss, there are no frills: just beautifully balanced rooms.

*Below* Breakfast room: steel and rushwork benches are cantilevered over a floating paranha pine floor with concealed lighting in channels on each side.

*Right* A dressing table in copper with stainless steel pivoting drawers hung on an unglazed mosaic wall.

*Above* Study with curved, stained, veneered desk cantilevered from a quarter-circular wall. Nineteen-fifties chair by Norman Cherner.

*Above* In this contemporary bathroom, the fittings are set against a free-standing, mosaic T-plan wall which isolates them from the original room.

*Above* This drawing room wall of natural sand and cement render punctuated with windows takes on the appearance of an abstract painting.

*Below* A polished plaster wall separates the drawing room from the staircase. The sofa is late18th-century English.

*Below* A sinuous lacquered wall lit from the floor creates the illusion of a curtain of wall hung from the ceiling.

*Above* A narrow dressing room with silk curtains to give richness; a day bed to lay out clothes; and a bathroom beyond.

*Below* Dressing corridor with mirrors to visually enlarge the narrow space. The bedroom is seen at the end of the corridor

# CHARLES RUTHERFOORD

## CHARLES RUTHERFOORD'S FIRST PRINCIPLES

- Don't be guided by the external walls. Make the interior space work for you.
- Use space between bedrooms and bathrooms as dressing areas. Coloured fabric hangings rather than hard finishes can be used to conceal clothes.
- Narrow spaces can be made to seem wider with mirrors, especially in dressing areas where mirrors are needed. A double bank of mirrors will create infinite reflections, though this may be too much for some tastes!
- Think how spaces relate to each other and the vista they will create when viewed from a distance.
- Divide space in a sculptural way to create new rooms without destroying the original space. Curved walls resemble screens and can be used to conceal a kitchen or a bathroom.
- Puncture walls to give views through to adjacent rooms, creating a layering effect. This will expand space and give it further dimension.
- Consider the appropriateness of colour and texture in relation to the architectural element on which you will use it.
- The junction of elements, either interlocking or set apart, will change the effect of a space.
- A floating wall with openings at either side to form entrances is an effective way to divide a large space. This works well around a chimney breast, although it is not always possible.

# CONTEMPORARY
# ARCHITECTURAL

# BAKER NEVILE

*Left* Lights set into the oak floor beneath the curtains give off a glow in the evenings. By day sunlight streams in through the pale silken curtains.

# BALANCE AND *SYMMETRY*

*Below* Before: the heavy curtains added warmth to cold evenings but made for a rather stifling room during the summer months.

Christopher Nevile and Justin Meath Baker don't just decorate rooms, they transform them into living spaces that say as much about the people who inhabit them as they do about the age in which we live. Their rooms are full of innovation, originality, excitement, wit and a youthful vitality that portrays them not only as designers, but also as artists. With a thorough understanding of architectural history, they bring a contemporary dimension to traditional and classical ideas, using modern materials while re-interpreting traditional techniques and crafts. As pioneers in design, they use artists and craftsmen to make all manner of furnishings which they display as artworks, often set on rugless hard floors and presented without over embellishment or covering up what is already beautiful. Cutting-edge interiors such as theirs are now practical in cold climates, as central heating has removed the need for the cosy warmth previously achieved through the use of heavy fabrics and rugs.

## FROM COSY TO CUTTING EDGE

The 'before' and 'after' photographs on this page show a drawing room in Fulham, London, that was totally transformed by Christopher and Justin to represent a whole new philosophy. The terraced house, built in the 1880s, was decorated in the 1980s in a cosy traditional style by the owner who, having grown out of that look, invited Baker Nevile to use their radical thinking and transform the room to reflect her own psychological move from the past to something more contemporary. The result is a beautiful tranquil interior far removed from its predecessor.

137

Heavy curtains and carpets in the previous scheme made the room warm and inviting in winter but rather overwhelming during the summer. With central heating and a gas log fire, the Baker Nevile scheme achieves a feeling of warmth while creating a light, airy environment during the summer months. The carpet has been replaced by a reclaimed oak floor, from Agora, London, in wide strips, limed to lighten the wood, and finished with a new skirting board painted in light, solid grey to sharpen the finish to the walls and floor. Curtains give off an ambient glow in the evenings, shimmering as the light dances through the silky fabric from the lights set into the floor. Simple blinds filter the daylight and shut out neighbours' eyes from the houses across the road, leaving no indication that the room is actually in a street in the heart of London.

PEELING AWAY THE PAST

Patterned wallpaper was removed to reveal the original plaster, which was then painted and waxed by specialists to resemble Italian stucco in a decaying palazzo. A line left behind when the dado was removed has been painted out, while the higher markings, remnants of a previous picture rail, have been retained to add a classical break to the wall finish, more in keeping with the proportions than the dado or chair rail. The cornice has been stripped of a hundred years of clogged paintwork to give it definition and form, but with a sensitivity to its history, so naked cracks are left exposed in order to enhance the notion of a time continuum. This is a

*Left* Before: a clutter of patterns, possessions and heirlooms.

*Right* After: a clean focus on the present, built on the bones of the past.

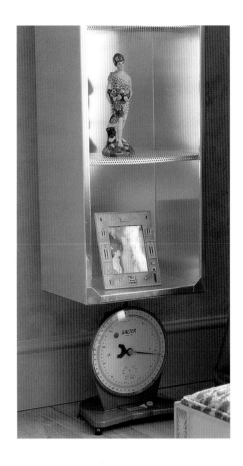

*Above* Aluminium boxes balanced on post-office scales house photographs and objects representing the weight of the client's past.

sophisticated approach to the idea of a room in transition and awaiting decoration, or of a life looking for meaning. In this instance, the stripping away of layers represents a departure from the past, whilst the exposure of the cracks alludes to the notion that one is forever in its shadow, and that to ignore the past is to deny it a real importance in our ability to move on to the next stage in life.

The many pictures on the walls were pared down to favourite images alone, giving them a focus that was previously blurred. Nevile suggested that the client purchase a set of four pictures to set above the marquetry table by David Linley. When she realized her budget only extended to one very small painting, Christopher came up with the ingenious idea of introducing an extremely large aluminium surround to the framed painting, giving it both presence and place within the context of the space as a whole. A set of prints of a European palace was taken away by Christopher Nevile and made into highly original leather-laced lampshades.

Family heirlooms, such as the gilded candle sconces, were not discarded but have taken on a new complexion in a contemporary environment. Likewise, the antique lyre-back chairs have been re-upholstered in bright apple green to add a zing to the colour scheme. The *chaise longue* contributes a little glamour without obscuring the curtains, and an old sofa, re-upholstered in linen, reveals legs that have been silver gilded. All these touches amply illustrate the ability of Christopher and Justin to incorporate detail into a total unity.

ARTWORKS AND INSTALLATIONS

Christopher and Justin enjoy the intellectual game of interacting with their clients to create an interior that says something about them through subtle representation. In this case, the free-standing display cabinets on either side of the fireplace contain personal items chosen by the owner to represent her past (shown above). The aluminium boxes are lit from the ceiling so that light shines through the perforated metal shelves, infusing the objects with a sense of weightlessness, so that the past hides, as it were, behind a veil of dappled light. A paradox immediately becomes apparent when one realizes that the shelves are perched on post-office scales, adding a touch of satire by registering the weight of the past. These cabinets would not be out of place in an art gallery.

The central glass-topped coffee table contains a collection of whimsical and ever-changing clutter that can be observed through the glass in the double-opening drawers without gathering dust. Here, it is the owner who becomes the artist.

# BAKER
# NEVILE

Although Christopher and Justin are full of new ideas, they never lose their respect for tradition. They use traditional ideas and transform them into a contemporary rhetoric. The two designers like to have fun and explore new avenues in design all the time, but nothing is done without a reason, however obscure that may be. In fact, they are closer to art than to mere decoration, and their meticulous attention to interior architecture transforms cornices, fireplaces and doorcases into features that set a scene.

## TRADITIONAL MEETS ETHNIC

At first sight, the entrance hall created for the British Interior Design Exhibition at Chelsea Old Town Hall, London (shown right), appears to be a straightforward exercise in traditional classicism based around an original William Kent fireplace. But on closer examination the room reveals a highly original contemporary statement. Gold leaf-edged architraves around the doors with jewel-like earrings on either side and, central to the pediment, a swirling disc in red glass with gold leaf, not only add ornamentation to the white room, but also form an almost ethnic relationship with the antique Oriental rug and the Indian elephant necklace on the classical 18th-century console table in an otherwise thoroughly British room.

*Above* The hallway created for the British Interior Design Exhibition at Chelsea Old Town Hall, London. Architectural features are transformed by touches of Eastern opulence, which add elements of surprise to a predominantly traditional room.

This approach has its rationale in history, because in the 18th and 19th centuries, British taste did incorporate collections and artifacts picked up from foreign travel, whether from the Grand Tour or through trading with the Empire. In this case, Christopher and Justin have relied upon the architecture to tell the story but they will often achieve a similar exotic result through the careful use of luxurious, colourful velvets, silks and linens used as touches of painterly detail within otherwise quite simple rooms.

Architectural elements, such as architraves, were created not only to hide the joint between the door frame and the plasterwork, but also as a form of decoration. Working with specialist craftsmen, Christopher and Justin turned these features into elements of household jewellery, carrying them beyond the usual interpretations by adding elements of surprise that smack of Eastern promise in an otherwise traditional room.

A chair and stool set before the Kent fireplace, designed by Christopher, are modern interpretations of traditional origin, covered in calico with brass tacks to define the elegant curve of the arms, with feet clad in pewter foil. The hallway is uncluttered by its simple furnishings while the exotic touches achieve a fascinating cohesion in what could have been a rather dull and formal waiting area. Here, the innovative mix of minimalism and opulence results in a highly original room that is full of the spiritual peace and calm of a welcoming resting place.

*Above* The fireplace in a country farmhouse in Lincolnshire, England, is given an almost baroque treatment as a piece of sculpture that dominates the room.

FIREPLACE OR SCULPTURE?

Nothing within any of their schemes should go unnoticed, as their success relies on the intellectual ideas behind the elements they develop to create a harmonious room to be lived in and enjoyed. One of their hallmarks is to turn a functional piece into a work of art. The fireplace, for example, is seen as the traditional focal point of a room and in their hands it can also become a contemporary art work. Historically, this is nothing new, but Christopher and Justin will, if appropriate, bring the concept into the present day.

A fireplace in a country farmhouse (shown above) was given an almost baroque treatment, resulting in a piece of sculpture that dominates the room. The ceiling is not particularly high and the fireplace, which is made of resin, plaster and wood and painted to look like carved stone, reaches to the ceiling, adding height to the room. Classical motifs are transformed from the expected pillars into tree trunks with sprouting branches and a unifying oak leaf relief in the central panel. With this substantial feature the room becomes focused so that the rest of the interior can succeed with simple decoration. Plain curtains dress small windows, hung high to gain maximum length. Traditionally grouped around the fireplace, the furniture falls into place without being at all contrived, and a subliminal warmth

emanates from the painted terracotta walls. A mix of contemporary and antique furniture, teamed with natural fabrics and textures, creates a relaxed yet stylish atmosphere.

*Above* The country kitchen in Lincolnshire, England where traditional and modern design elements are seamlessly combined.

## SIMPLICITY AND SURPRISES

The kitchen of the same house (shown above), looks perfectly traditional at first glance. However, one notices subtle touches in the details, such as the bejewelled light fittings made by artist Catherine Purves. Here, the fireplace treatment is a pared-down version of the fireplace in the sitting room, giving continuity within the house in a different guise. Simplicity is paramount, so the mirror is set into the wall as an effective device to marry the overmantle with the base.

*Right and below*
Bedroom and
bathroom in the
eaves of a country
manor house.

## OPENING THE SPACE

Devoid of any form of embellishment, the bedroom (shown above) set in
the eaves of an old country house shows the ultimate Baker Nevile
interpretation of simplicity without austerity. Originally a low-ceilinged
maid's room, the roof space has been opened up to form the principal
bedroom. The bed is a commissioned piece made from salvaged medieval
oak beams and dressed with sheer cotton voile that forms a canopy from
the crossbeam that supports the ceiling. Being quite high off the ground, the
bed has a step ladder at the base, which also acts as a table for books. There
is a separate bathroom (shown left) and dressing room, which leaves the
bedroom unencumbered, with discreet lighting hidden among the beams.
The bathroom is in the same open, pared down style as the bedroom.

# BAKER
# NEVILE

*Right* Bath treatment: the bath resembles a stage set, with open curtains in front, producing a proscenium arch.

*Below left and right* Bathroom in a London apartment in Mayfair – modern drama in 18th-century dress.

*Above* The bedroom is pared down to a more simple form, complementing the dramatic bathroom.

## CONTRASTING APARTMENTS

The bathroom in a Mayfair apartment (shown left) is an interpretation of modern drama in 18th-century dress. A *grisaille* wallpaper panel of classical erotic imagery by Zubber, *Psyche au bain*, is reflected into the room, echoed in the linoleum floor, the *trompe l'oeil* drapery behind the bath and the frieze on the cornice and the bath panel. The exotic decoration is executed in tones of sober grey with painted borders to unify and frame all the architectural elements. Here, the bath resembles a stage set with open curtains in front, creating a proscenium arch. The bedroom (shown above) complements the bathroom but is pared down to a simpler form, featuring only a bed, a piano, a fire, a modern floor lamp and polished oak boards. Finally, the vast wall space is articulated with simple painted panelling and nothing but a simple, square mirror.

# BAKER
# NEVILE

By way of complete contrast, the north London bathroom (shown below) is shaped by the walls themselves. Solid, curved shapes have been been given polished finishes to emphasize their lines. This room was an awkward shape, so Christopher and Justin decided to turn this to their advantage by curtaining the bath and creating a cocoon within for the bather. The door handle by Matthew Hilton is, in fact, an ashtray and is the only decorative feature in the stark room, which is otherwise the epitome of simplicity. Detailing in the edging to the stone vanity basin and the line to the curved bath emphasize a horizontal dimension to the vertical lines.

The *en suite* bedroom is another room dictated by its architecture, and works in perfect harmony with the adjacent bathroom. Chunky columns, which conceal air conditioning, hi-fi and CDs, frame the far wall and flanking mirrors extend the space, giving the illusion of further rooms while reflecting the light from the windows opposite, which look out onto a small balcony. The plain, light walls are unadorned except for a single picture placed squarely above the bed, while the television is fixed high on the wall to keep furniture to a minimum.

Both schemes are reactions to quite different briefs. Each represents comfort, both visually and literally, but neither is comfortable in the conventional, bourgeois sense. They are both artistic, honest expressions of the functions that are their purpose, thought-provoking as balanced compositions and full of intellectual stimulation.

*Left* Bedroom, Abbey Road, London; a calm, uncluttered interior.

*Right* Bathroom, Abbey Road – a minimalist approach that is dictated by the architecture.

147

# BAKER
# NEVILE

### AN ELEMENTAL SWIMMING POOL

The swimming pool room Baker Nevile designed for The Design House, Cambrige Gate, explores the elements: earth, fire, air and water. A stainless steel pool transforms into a dance floor when the square-panelled glass floor rises up through the water at the touch of a button – the ultimate in transformable space.

There is an abundance of light from the vast, restored Edwardian skylight, and by night, fibre optics glisten through the water and glow from behind the architraves and the fire surround. A mirrored fireplace is as much a surreal framed picture as a functional fire with flames that reflect on the water at night. The shape of the glass panels in the pool floor, taken from the grid in the skylight, have been re-interpreted again in Baker Nevile's design of the slate and wood floor, an obvious modern intrusion into this traditional space. Even the gas log fire – in itself a falsification – is a deliberate comment in its ability to summon up fire at the flick of a switch.

### A RADICAL APPROACH

Christopher and Justin have an ever-evolving style, which adapts to the people and spaces that they have worked with, and responds to and grows around their clients. The post-modern age has made anything possible or acceptable in design, with no one style to follow. Early in his career, Christopher was creating rooms in keeping with the English country house look, but now, moving in leaps and bounds, he and Justin have influenced design with their more radical approach without losing an affection for traditional ideas. They represent an exciting contribution to the development of the future of interior design.

*Right* The swimming pool in the basement of The Design House, Cambridge Gate, becomes an exploration of the elements: earth, fire, air and water.

# BAKER NEVILE

BAKER NEVILE'S FIRST PRINCIPLES

- Ignore the notion of taste.
- Question everything and voice your ideas, however crazy they may sound.
- Every scheme should have a hook to hang your ideas on – a story or plot which revolves around the room or house. This could be inspired by the building, a picture, perhaps a piece of furniture or a favourite poem.
- If an element doesn't help to tell the story, then don't use it. Be ruthless and stick to the plot, like all good storytellers.
- Rooms must be allowed to evolve and change, adapt and grow. They must be able to change with you, so don't be too precious. Like us, interiors are transitory.
- Commission as much as you can – it is more fun, you are more involved and the finished result is more personal. Become a patron so that the applied arts can survive.

# PETER WADLEY

## STATE OF
## *THE ART*

For Peter Wadley, interior architecture is as much about the relationship his clients will form with their living space as with the physical relationship between rooms, surfaces and textures. He believes that the ease and excitement his architecture brings should be on a par with the comfort and stimulation afforded by the company of friends. Peter's designs result from a careful understanding of the client and their brief, the function required from the building and his own ability to enjoy design problems as they arise. It is an evolving process, and the enthusiastic involvement of his clients, both intellectually and emotionally, feeds and feeds off his imagination. Peter aims to develop an architecture that feels physically good to the occupant, one that makes relevant, if sometimes surprising connections between the user and the world beyond.

### PLAYING GAMES WITH PLACE, SPACE AND TIME

For decades, interior design has been viewed as cushions, covers and decorative finishes to achieve a 'look'. Today, design has far more to do with the 18th-century 'patron/client' role than ever before. From the beginning, Peter seeks to develop an empathy with his client, the client's needs and wants, and the site itself. His intention is to use these elements to develop a concept, or a series of conceits, that will transcend the physical, emotional and intellectual facets of the project and make a whole.

No detail is ever incorporated without a purpose or meaning. Often the meanings are personal to the clients, resulting in a subtle iconography that brings the space alive. Peter likes to encourage patrons of his work to have

# PETER
# WADLEY

fun, and help them to open their minds to a plethora of possibilities, often changing the way in which they live or perceive themselves. The final result will always convey something that is confident and forward-thinking about them to their friends and visitors, giving their lifestyle a new dimension.

## THE MEWS MUSE

For The Design House, Cambridge Gate, Peter was given eighty-seven square metres of empty space on the ground floor of the mews house in which to incorporate changing rooms, showers, toilets, two bed-sitting rooms, a steam room and a staircase. In this case, he had no direct client with whom to develop ideas for the scheme. It was by chance that the best floor plan for the bed-sitting rooms, changing rooms and steam room (shown on these and the previous pages) formed itself into a shape that resembled a fragment of the flank of a giant 'Muse'. Here, the meanings of the word allowed Peter a sculptural and pictorial program relating to the crazy richness of phonetics and meaning in the English language.

The circulation space, the museum, was formed against an undulating wall that follows the lines in plan of the female muse. The wall is covered with a digital inkjet mural, created by artist Martin Fuller to conceal the service rooms behind it (shown on page 150). The imagery is all about mutation (another derivative of the meaning of muse) and the relationships of muses and men in space. The shape of the muse is developed further in an abstract way, with her 'belt' bursting through Fuller's mural to hold the champagne bar (shown on page 150) and lead the bather into the changing rooms (shown above left) and steam room (shown right), all of which are contained within her 'corset'. Mirrors inside the muse (shown right) reflect her half-figure to make her whole, and there is a progression of different hues in the changing rooms (shown above left), the little toilet and the steam room with twinkling fibre-optic lights. The changing rooms are coded red for 'port' and green for 'starboard' to remind us that all are blessed who sail in this vessel!

## ALLUSIONS AND ILLUSIONS

As a modernist architect, Peter demonstrates in this series of rooms and spaces a simple use of lighting, vibrant contrasting textures of stone, etched glass, metalwork, colour and commissioned art works, together with a vocabulary of spatial and iconographic games that transcend function. The glass door that leads through the curved wall is etched with the meanings of muse and mews, giving a hint of what the composition is all about. The corridor created by the mural, lit with fibre-optic lights set into the floor,

*Above left* Port and starboard changing rooms are contained within the corset of the muse.

*Below left* A hawk on its perch, central to the composition, sits on the staircase that drops through strata to the orangery and garages below.

*Right* Steam room saturated in graduated blue mosaic by Mosaik, star-spangled with fibre-optics by Absolute Action.

*Below* Starboard changing room with stainless steel column casings by Rimex.

incorporates the bar unit that arrives between the full-length windows, attached to the service rooms by a wooden ceiling section that represents the muse's belt.

A carved hawk by Julian Stanley (shown on page 152), is a representation of the original mews occupants before the conversion into stables. Perched above the stairs, the hawk's reflection looks out from the mirrors.

The welded steel model of the ballroom and pool on the floor above, by Matthew Livsey-Hammond, is strapped to the back of the metaphorical muse, alluding to the baggage of history and decoration that this contemporary torch-bearer has to carry. A narrow staircase to the garage and the orangery below is reflected three times in the mirrored walls, becoming very grand and central as it drops through to the basement below. It is protected by ten miniature muses in painted steel, which support the etched glass balustrade. Peter's game is not always obvious, but it is present in all his projects and is the concept that makes his spaces and rooms hang together.

## MASTERFUL USE OF MIRROR

The bedroom suite created for a house in Fulham, London, was originally one room with three windows. By cutting the room at the third window, Peter incorporated a bathroom and walk-in closet without making the bedroom appear much smaller. Removing the chimney breast gave the bathroom eight extra inches of all-important space to fit the bath in without stealing too much space from the bedroom. The sliding mirrored doors disappear when opened, behind the arched central wall section (shown above far right), leading the eye to a view of the bathroom and dressing room beyond, and giving the illusion of space at all times. When closed, the doors offer a double reflection of the room on either side (shown right).

The bathroom is masterful. An arched wall section, or dolmen, as Peter calls it, built in the bedroom is a fragment of the wall at the back of the bathroom, 'pulled out' to support the neo-classical vanity unit in the

bedroom, designed by Anthony Paine, that functions as dressing table and wash-basin. This is an illusionary architectural game that controls detailing, and is so carefully constructed that the back of the dolmen, (shown right), is made to fit precisely into the back shelving around the end of the bath, where display shelves of shells and starfish are inset with cupboard space above the concealed cistern. Both ends of the bath are lit with downlights, the bedroom end making use of the alcove for a heated towel rail. The large

*Below* The 'dolmen' floats in the mirrored space supporting the elegant Biedermeier-style wash-stand.

*Above* The bathroom-side of the dolmen arches over the dividing wall to the dressing room.

*Below right* The 'real' view back into the bedroom, as can be seen from the bathroom.

*Above* In the bathroom, the central dividing wall separating the dressing room holds the Biedermeier mirror.

mirror and bath unit, also designed by Anthony Paine, reflects the light from the window and a view to enjoy while lying in the marble-clad bath. The walls surrounding the dolmen are covered with mirror at both sides so that both bedroom and bathroom ceiling and cornice are reflected to give the illusion of greater space. Mirror runs above the neo-classical wall mirror, giving the illusion that the half-constructed arch is equal in size to the arched wall in the bedroom. When the sliding bathroom door is open, hidden within the arched dolmen, the rooms open up to see reality, the bedroom becoming an extension of the bathroom (shown right).

The colour scheme is simple, allowing the Biedermeier-style furniture designed by Anthony Paine to give strength, adding soft hues of blue and putty pink taken from the linen curtains from Benison Fabrics. Flaming torches and a curtain pole from Mark Brazier-Jones support the bedhead by Jon Rhodes. Neo-classical accessories give equilibrium to architectural furniture, they are new and modern yet inspired by traditional ideas. Few pictures are displayed, but each one adds to the relationship between furniture and detailing, a rapport that is regarded as synonymous with all of Peter's work.

# PETER
WADLEY

SAWING UP

Peter gave a four-storey 1840s terraced house (shown on these pages) radical treatment, creating space that transcends all barriers. The house has steps up to the front door on the ground floor, and had a low ceiling in the garden floor space below with separate entrance. His brief was to create a living space onto the garden, conducive to simple, informal entertaining, incorporating a sitting room, dining room, office and kitchen. With almost too many rooms for his bachelor client to inhabit, Peter suggested that the sitting room area on the garden floor be given double height, incorporating a huge, double-hung sash window, so the two floors would inter-relate and the balcony on the upper floor would communicate with the space below. In this way, all the rooms are walked through on the way to bed.

The handrail is made from polished stainless steel with balustrading and circular-saw washers in lacquered mild steel that together represent the cutting edge of a metaphoric saw that has cut the hole through the joists and boards of the original floor (shown far right). A glass lectern (shown below and far right) with its torch support, crashes into the handrails to act as a butler's tray to put things on when opening the conservatory door beyond, or perhaps a place from which to harangue visitors arriving below!

*Below* Ground floor introduction to the new living space. The hole is protected by the 'saw' balustrade and contained by the huge, double-hung sash window and double-storey chimney breast.

*Above right* The garden floor sitting room showing the double-hung sash window, a butler's table and torch.

*Below right* A long view down the lower floor room, showing the recessed structural beam that has been transformed into a linear chandelier.

The triangular fan in the ceiling pushes heat back down into the lower room, a decorative feature that replaces the ornate chandelier of traditional schemes. A double sash window provides an impressive amount of light to both floors and relieves the effect of the compressed ceiling on the lower floor. The lighting (shown below) is recessed into the ceiling in V-shapes sparkling with 10-volt capsule lamps, reminiscent of the owner's initial and the geometry of the balustrade saw.

Peter uses a radiator to form the balustrade to the stairs to the garden level, painted to continue the panelling of the under-stair cupboards, and places a reclaimed cast-iron column as a giant newel post at the bottom. The rooms are unified by the maple boards that run throughout the garden level and accommodate a dining table at one end, a slate work bench along the side wall and a sitting area, thus giving the multi-function space a variety of purpose.

At night the room resembles a medieval hall with its lacquered steel shutter bars, the fan, the saw and the giant newel post. The space becomes a great room, painted in off-white to contrast with the grey of the metal and the yellow of the floor, the low-voltage lights creating a modest atmosphere of reverence, serenity and calm.

# PETER WADLEY

BIG HOUSE, LITTLE HOUSE

A house in Vermont was sited by Peter on a ridge to offer views of mountain ranges from the north-east to the south-west. In this case, the context and brief called for a traditional, classic building related to the Vermont vernacular architecture of connected farmhouses (shown below left) and the contemporary requirement for a centralized great room for ease of modern living.

The New England farm structure of big house, little house, back house and barn, formed as a solution to the problems of a harsh climate, growing families, plus the effects of gradual modernization and extensions over time. It was agreed between the client, the builder and Peter that there should be a Federal-style house at the 'front'. Standing on the ridge, this Federal house, which, true to tradition is orientated due south, can be seen from afar (shown right).

The road to the property winds up past the Federal house into the mud yard at the rear where the

*Opposite page, anti-clockwise from top* The contemporary classic New England Federal house designed by Peter hovers just above the pond.

A traditional New England farm which provided the inspiration for the contemporary building.

The sheltering porch cuts off at a 45-degree angle to catch two views.

The great room that grows out of the back of the Federal house is partially engulfed by the carriage wing and forms the sheltering porch roof to the north-east.

A three-quarter view of the Federal house, with the added buildings behind.

*Right* The view south into the great room from the carriage wing gallery showing triple-hung sash windows.

agricultural forms of the silo and the carriage ell (wing) define the three entrances (shown below right opposite). The everyday mudroom (the room entered from the yard) door leads into the carriage wing on the left, while the main front door with its European porch nestles into the silo at the centre of the composition. A path to the right leads down to what will be the terraced lawn, and round to the Federal house door.

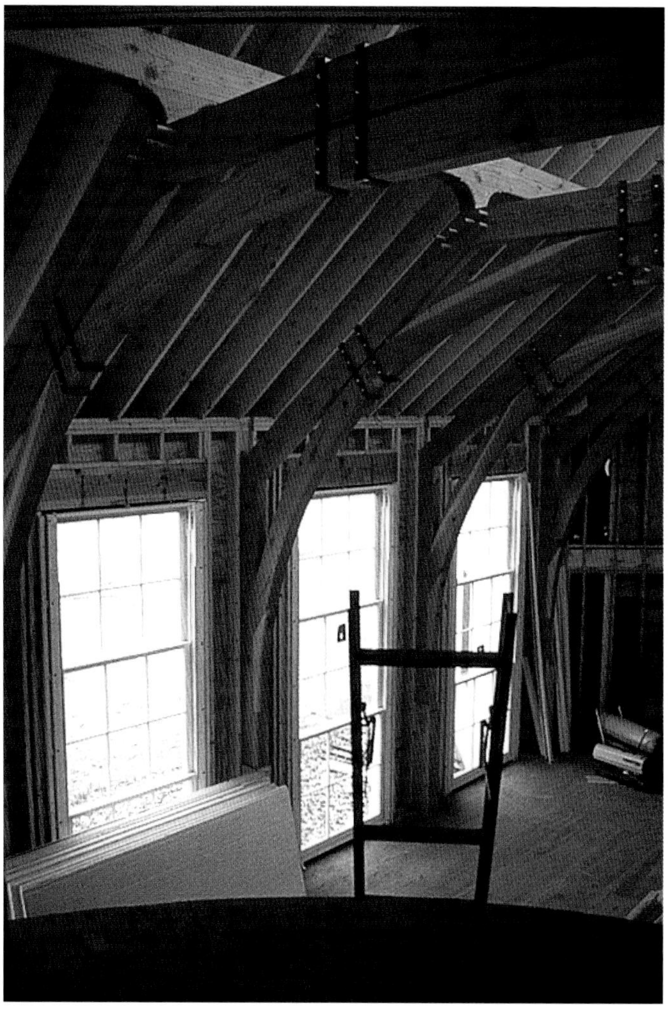

The silo, which contains bathrooms, is positioned immediately behind the Federal house and provides the pivot for the new geometry and style of the great room. The latter grows out of the back of the Federal house, and collides with the carriage wing, which contains the kitchen and serves the great room.

## ROOM WITH A VIEW

The great room is controlled by its chimney and two staircases that drop into it from balconies on the Federal house to the south and the carriage wing to the north. The balconies from the carriage wing and the Federal house speak to each other across the space. The room almost feels like an outside area, with windows from the silo and a little squint window from the master bedroom looking down into it. Four triple-hung sash windows look out to the view to the south-east, while the space of the great room breaks out towards the mountains to the north-east.

The roof wing, or sheltering porch (shown below left opposite), is cut off at 45 degrees to catch the two views. Bold timber arches and purlins support the roof, split with roof lights to catch the evening sun and orient the room. The exterior materials are traditional: painted clapboard, shingles and vertical siding with a slate roof. Inside, solid wood floors are used for rooms, slate and limestone for service areas, and walls and ceilings are of simple painted plaster. The casings and mouldings are New England Puritan, as perfectly befits an area once settled by the Shakers.

*Above* A ladder leads up to a trap door through which lies a spare bedroom.

*Above* The hanging ceiling in this kitchen space is the floor of the study above.

*Above* A bungalow converted into a 'new' villa, Hampshire, England.

*Below* Built-in cupboards installed in this 1840s London house contain an oblique reference to the New York sky line.

*Below* The interior of this shower has mirrors opposite each other forming an endless reflection.

*Right* A concealed structural beam in the double-level garden room deforms the ceiling and is de-materialized with mirror and a linear chandelier.

*Below* The band-saw balustrade, with its circular-saw washers and a long slate work bench along the wall behind.

# PETER WADLEY

## PETER WADLEY'S FIRST PRINCIPLES

- Use an architect or a designer. Do the leg work to find out their design philosophy before you decide to work with them.

- Allow your designer to play creative leap-frog with you. It is good to participate and helps them to move on!

- Do let your designer innovate. The use of materials and technology should be relevant to the problem and not dictated by fashion. Their choice should evolve with the development of the project concept and conceits.

- Buildings are not there just to keep the rain out but also to expand the mind. Things only get to sing when the practicality of the brief is provided for within a relevant concept linking your efforts to your culture.

- Most spaces are controlled, one way or another, by circulation routes, which are in their turn controlled by symbolic formal elements such as front doors, staircases, chimney stacks etc. Get the circulation route right, and in doing so the formal elements will fall into place.

- The development of detail needs to relate totally to the controlling concepts and conceits for a scheme to hang together. Often, the detailing will alter a concept. You need to stay in control while being light on your feet.

- Buildings are boxes to protect us from the elements and myriad other attacks. We develop systems for supporting them, clothing them, getting in and out of them. These are related historically to our technology which, inconveniently, changes all the time. Be brave and decide where you are.

- All design, whatever the scale, has to go through the same process of analysis, synthesis, building and enjoyment. The process is unavoidable, so enjoy it and feed your experience to take your scheme on.

# STEPHEN RYAN

# ARCHITECTURAL
# *SOPHISTICATION*

*Left* Stephen Ryan's neo-classical drawing room in an 1860s London townhouse is a harmonious symphony on the theme of white. Textures bring variety, from the marble features of Juno to the leather chairs, the textured wool rug and the damask Tuscan blind.

Stephen Ryan has had an almost unique training as apprentice and protégé to David Hicks, the founder of the British classical contemporary interior. Acclaimed as 'student of the year' at the Inchbald School of Design, Stephen was hand picked by David Hicks to work for him. During this time he gained the knowledge and experience that has enabled him to develop his own ideas into a Hicks vernacular. It was an education that taught him not to discard the past but to bring it forward into the modern age, adhering to the Hicks rules of symmetry, architectural order and the careful use of a classical language within a contemporary theme.

Early on in his career, Stephen learned that the essence that made an interior read as 'contemporary' could be achieved in a room full of antique furniture and pictures by carefully incorporating modern touches. Frequently, he will design modern classical frames for 18th- and 19th-century prints, adding prominence and stature to the art works, while bringing them forward into the context of a new environment. Stephen is adept in creating living spaces that will enrich the lives of those who live in them, while projecting their own ethos to the outside world.

## CLASSICAL SYMMETRY

There is a unique fluidity about Stephen's rooms, which come about through a complementary process that usually starts with a colour palette, often chosen to meld with particular pieces or fabrics. The room shown left follows the creams and whites of the classical sculpture, giving an understated emphasis to the monumental head and vases, placed centrally

163

on a substantial table, which itself defines the window beyond. The table display is a perfect example of symmetry, which to Stephen is integral to harmony. He has the ability to incorporate classicism in such a way that it transcends nostalgia and becomes representative of the modern era. Serenity, calm, peace and order have been composed into a private domain away from the chaos of the outside world. The inhabitants will inevitably bring their own colour and life to the scene, creating within it the ambience of their choice.

At first sight the room may look like a formal 'set piece'. However, the formality is only subliminal, coming from a homage to classical ideals. The spiritual quality in the room is drawn from subconscious intellectual references: the table set in the form of an altar-piece, the head of the goddess Juno and the ecclesiastical candles are all informed by our own understanding of worship. It is not conducive to kneeling and praying, but gives out an aura that is tranquil and spiritual without being at all religious. There is nothing pretentious about the room – it is understated by virtue of the monochromatic scheme, but rich in texture, pattern and shape.

The candles, on their tall, slim, metalwork bases, are like the columns of an architectural order, framing the head and adding a kinetic orange glow to the creamy tones at night. Stephen has designed every detail: the stone-topped table, the carpet, the chairs and the side table, using his design skills to create a perfect composition. Like Hicks, Stephen prefers to design the main elements that contribute to his compositions, enabling him to create a 'haute couture' result that is so often required by his clients.

## A STILL LIFE

The way in which rooms read, one to another, is all-important to Stephen. The bathroom door (shown right) when open frames the chest of drawers in the hallway, which is symmetrically set with *objets d'art* and flanked by a pair of pictures with a plaster relief over the central mirror. It is a still life, lit with tall, slim candlestick lamp bases, a style that comes directly from David Hicks, as a break from cumbersome bases and shades. The tablescape, composed of architectural elements, an original Japanese print and an Indian head, displays Stephen's eclecticism, which is always a strong trait in his design schemes.

The bathroom itself is deliberately designed without the symmetrical pairing of the hallway beyond. Here, Stephen applies a balance that is both harmonious and functional. His use of candles, placed on the edge of the wash-basin, shows his concern that atmosphere should be regarded as an important consideration in every room of the house.

*Above* A view of the hallway, as seen from the gentleman's bathroom.

*Above* Bathing alcove in the dramatic bed-sitting room. The side tables, sofa and fabrics were all designed by Stephen Ryan; the candlelamps are by David Hicks.

## ONE-ROOM LIVING

His bed-sitting room for the British Interior Design Exhibition at Chelsea Old Town Hall, London is a masterful use of space and an inspiration to anyone seeking a grand *pied à terre* with all that is needed for civilized living in one room (shown above). Stephen makes full use of the large space, concealing a bath behind curtains and a wash-basin and kitchenette inside cupboards. The high ceiling and good dimensions gave him a wide berth to set about creating a new symmetry within the space.

At each corner he has designed average-height cupboards on catch openers, extending them upwards to fit the space by incorporating pieces of contemporary sculpture, lit in the void as art displays and framed with a circle of gold leaf to draw the eye upwards and add decoration (shown above). The cornice, taken right around the room, is brought in front of the bath to create a self-contained alcove. Bevelled mirror panels on the interior walls and ceiling of the bath alcove are lit from above and act like the facets of a diamond, radiating light, controlled by a dimmer.

Touches of muted gold and brass catch the eye with a fluidity that passes from the picture and sculpture frames, overdoors, lamps and Napoleonic emblems to the bath panel, brass studs on the chair and television table (which rotates) to the cross bars on the cupboard doors. A spotlight shines through the glass shelves to the left of the bath, defusing through the glazed levels to add further moodiness to the scene.

There were no architectural features in the room at the outset, giving Stephen the chance to start from scratch and design the door frames with simple, mahogany edging articulated with gold squares to define plaster reliefs in the pediments above as framed pictures. These, together with the

*Above* Bed alcove opposite the bathing alcove in the bed-sitting room. The lamps, rug, bed and swivel television unit were all designed by Stephen Ryan. A Montgolfier chandelier and intimate dining for two complete this romantic room. "Very Violetta, very *Traviata*," as Ryan called it.

fabric behind the cupboard doors, break up the heavy mahogany woodwork and dark fabric-covered walls to lighten and brighten the room.

The *lit bateau*, designed by Stephen, acts as a bed or a sofa, with drawers underneath for storage. A fabric corona makes a cosy cocoon of dark red lining. His colour palette is simple, taking the beige and white fabric of the bath curtains and bed dressing into the rug and sofa to contrast with the dark walls and heavy upholstery. The dark red of the corona lining is carried through to the ruched trim, the border of the central rug, the upholstery fabrics and the paintwork inside the cupboards.

Nothing is overdone or created without a purpose. Tall, slim lamps and a balloon candle chandelier by Kevin McCloud cut into the empty middle space between the furniture and the ceiling, becoming essential features to such a high-ceilinged room. A slate floor acts as an undefined hallway and separates the area from the rug that marks out the sitting area. The total effect here is seductive, masculine, original and also very welcoming.

## DIAMOND PANELS

Once a designer has an idea that works, we see him use it in different guises. Inspired by the cupboards in the bedsit, Stephen created a bedroom in light oak (shown below), taking a diamond relief into the door panels, edged in mahogany, with frames that evolved from the architraves in his bedsit. The door detail (shown right) reveals a skirting board with a band of turned rope incorporated to reflect the owner's interest in sailing.

*Above* Beautifully executed joinery detail in a London penthouse.

*Left* A glamorous bedroom in a London penthouse, featuring silk wall- and bed-hangings and Brussels-weave carpeting.

# STEPHEN RYAN

SOFT AS SILK

The lilac and beige bedroom designed for The Design House, Cambridge Gate (shown on these pages) is similar in colour palette to the bedsit, yet far more feminine. Stephen designed the damask cut-and-loop textured wool carpet and used plain beige gauffraged (stamped) simulated suede cloth to add softness to the fireplace wall, cleverly framing the mirror and creating a shape in keeping with the four-poster bed dressing.

The soft lilac cotton chintz damask on the bed is lined with fabrics in apricot, vanilla, mocha and celadon, making a colourful tent over a simple metal frame, the fabric held back with silk and crystal beaded tie-backs hung on glass finials which mirror the Lalique crystal ornaments in the room. The television is masterfully hidden within a plinth which rotates to

*Below* A Moderne style bedroom evoking all the essential glamour of French 1930s style. Bedside table, lamps, carpet and the *Brook* damask fabric all designed by Stephen Ryan.

*Above* An antique chair covered with pony skin sits in front of a classic Regency-style chimney piece. The *fer forge* side table by Stephen Ryan supports a vase by Lalique.

*Above* Here three wardrobe areas with a central decorative niche are used to give architectural symmetry to this open dressing room.

*Above* Taupe ultra-suede is used for curtains and stretched onto walls and wardrobe doors. The custom-designed wardrobe is a plinth for a *Sèvres* vase.

reveal the television when required or, when turned to the wall, acts as a stylish fluted column displaying a piece of sculpture.

A pair of cupboards at either side of the fireplace have suede panels reflecting the tones in the lining fabrics used for the bed curtains, co-ordinating all the colours that make up the basic palette. The patterns and textures are exquisite: from the fabrics and the embossed carpet, to the fur bedspread and the jade beads that dangle from the bedside lampshade. No detail has been neglected and the room exudes the glamour, colours and femininity of the 1930s.

The walls are covered in ultra-suede, a soft fabric with leaf-pattern relief in subtle shades of mink, and protected from picture-hanging damage by a thin picture rail device running under the cornice with nylon wires to position pictures as required. Here, the lack of symmetrical proportions was such that it was impossible for Stephen to place the bed against the wall, so he positioned it in the middle and played with the space around it. At one end he has created an open

# STEPHEN RYAN

*Right* A feminine bathroom featuring white opaque glass walls from Rankins (Glass) Company, white thassos marble surfaces and custom-designed *verre eglomisé* mirror.

*Below* Matisse-inspired shower enclosure with a frameless glass wall, designed by Stephen Ryan.

dressing area, lined in wide bevelled strips of mirror to conceal jib doors at either side, leading to a 'his' and 'her' shower room and bathroom.

In the feminine bathroom (shown above) Stephen uses light colours in a fabric from Manuel Canovas for a simple curtain. This design is repeated in the *verre eglomisé* silvered panels behind the bath. The walls are lined in opaque glass, popular in the 1930s.

In contrast, the masculine shower room (shown left) is dark with black opaque glass, marble, slate and black textured paper and set off with strong directional lighting. The drama of the chiaroscuro is brought to life by Stephen's design for the architectural mirror frame in sycamore and ebony, and the striking mosaic, after Matisse, created by Donna Reeves. Stephen is a master of dramatic contrasting effects that are almost a mirror image of each other.

The room shown right is equally brilliant and conveys a style that is neither masculine nor feminine.

*Above* Classic symmetry in neo-Regency taste with a Brussels-weave carpet, Thomas Hope-style table and classical chairs designed by Stephen Ryan. The obelisk bookcases are by David Hicks and the chandelier originates from the estate of Stephen Tennant.

Stephen's daring use of pink might have communicated femininity, but with the heavy mahogany obelisk cabinets the colour is equalized and diluted. Symmetry is evident in the pairs of display cabinets, chairs, sofas and lamps, unified by the central chandelier and table, after the 18th-century cabinetmaker Thomas Hope. The carpet, in hues of greys and whites, demonstrates the merits of a well-designed patterned carpet. Prior to pioneers in this field, such as Hicks and John Fowler, patterned carpets were used to avoid the appearance of stains in pubs and inns and, by association, became an anathema to the visually literate, starting a dull trend for the plain, safe carpet. Today, in complete contrast to this, designers are more inclined to use patterned carpet as a visual enhancement.

*Above left* An extension to a country house features a new conservatory-style dining room. Here, crisp, white joinery offsets the terracotta-coloured polished plaster walls.

*Middle left* A corner of a traditional English-style country house. Faded Bennison fabrics with silk linen upholstered walls are underscored with a silk taffeta-covered table.

*Below left* This attractive blue and white themed guest bedroom in a London penthouse has carefully chosen accessories.

*Below* Five 18th-century Greek merchant's houses have been converted into a luxurious hotel. This picture shows the themed 'house of portraits'.

*Above right* Graphically cool, this masculine bedroom is decorated with witty wallpaper designed by Karl Lagerfeld. Grey flannel curtains form part of a strict black and white colour palette.

*Below right* A small dining room in London features these unusual celadon fake-pigskin walls and upholstery.

## STEPHEN RYAN'S FIRST PRINCIPLES

■ Start with a basic overall colour and add a variety of patterns in similar tones. For dramatic schemes, use a dark base and punctuate it with lighter accessories and patterns.

■ Use dark, dramatic schemes in rooms with little natural light.

■ In small rooms, tone the window treatment to match the walls.

■ Have less furniture in small rooms but choose oversized pieces to create a feeling of space.

■ Use plain silvered mirror with conviction: mirrors are a great space enlarger.

■ Use mirrors on window reveals to bounce light back into dark rooms.

■ Hang curtains as high as possible to add height to the room.

■ If there is dead space between the window and cornice, hang blinds to cover the space, giving an impression of a much larger window.

■ Ugly views are best concealed by filtering devices such as perforated roller blinds that let in light while obscuring the view. Alternatively, use Venetian blinds in either metal or wood or classical colonial shutters on the inside.

■ Hard floors are tiring on the feet. Soften them with rugs and warm them with underfloor heating.

■ If you must put rugs over carpet, ensure that the fitted carpet is plain with a low pile. Natural floor coverings are preferable.

■ Use lampshades with covered tops or crown-silvered light bulbs to direct light downwards and to avoid haloes all over the ceiling.

■ If space permits, use oversized lampbases to add proportion and a sculptural element.

■ Plagiarize ideas from previous centuries.

■ Use concealed (jib) doors leading to anterooms, bathrooms or dressing rooms to give greater symmetry within a space.

# DESIGN
# *DIRECTORY*

Having worked with over two thousand highly efficient and competent suppliers to the interior design industry over a period spanning more than fifteen years during my British Interior Design Exhibitions, it was difficult to make a small selection to be represented within this book. I have tried to choose companies that meet the needs of both interior designers and private clients in various useful categories.

Interior designers are only as good as the suppliers and craftsmen that they employ to contribute to their design scheme, and I hope that the companies described in the following pages will prove to be useful recommendations. The smaller companies offer a highly personal service and the larger manufacturers are able to service almost any requirement. Many of these companies are based in the United Kingdom but work all over the world; others have agencies abroad. Many of them will have portfolios or catalogues that can be requested.

I know from experience that reliable sources are always hard to find, so each company listed here comes with my highest recommendation.

*Fleur Rossdale*

## FABRICS AND WALLPAPERS

### BRIAN LAWRENCE LIMITED

Brian Lawrence Limited design and supply classical furniture, fabrics and accessories.

The company also design and market for Bennett silks and Borderline fabrics, Devoré cushions and accessories, Philip Hooper Design Associates and Mangani Porcelaine.

The cherub fabric shown below was designed by Philip Hooper and Brian Lawrence and is available in five colourways with a complementary trellis design. Philip Hooper Design Associates also design and supply cabinet, upholstered and garden furniture.

44 Dartford Road,
Sevenoaks,
Kent TN13 3TQ
tel: 01732 741 308
fax: 01732 450 122

### BRUNSCHWIG & FILS

Founded in France in 1900, Brunschwig & Fils has become world famous for the quality of their classic decorative fabrics, wallpapers, trimmings, upholstered furniture, tables, lamps and mirrors.

10 The Chambers,
Chelsea Harbour Drive,
London SW10 0XF
tel: 0171 351 5797
fax: 0171 351 2280

US contact:
Brunschwig & Fils
75 Virginia Road,
North White Plains,
NY 10603-0905
tel: 914 684 5800

### LELIEVRE (UK) LTD

LeLievre and Tassinari & Chatel have been weavers of fine fabrics since 1680. Their collection of plain silks, damasks, brocades and velours are woven at the mills in the Lyon area in the French midlands.

LeLievre have a large collection of velours which include plains, striped, checks, and printed designs. There is also a substantial collection of designs which can be gaufraged onto the velours and most other fabrics as well.

1/19 Chelsea Harbour
Design Centre,
London
SW10 0XE

US contact:
Old World Weavers
D & D Building,
979 Third Avenue,
New York
NY 10022
tel: 212 355 7186

### MARVIC TEXTILES LTD

Marvic Textiles, recognized for over fifty years as a leading designer of furnishing fabrics, offer a comprehensive range of 'modern classics' specializing in upholstery weaves, chenilles, silks, damasks, moirés, toiles de jouy, crewels and linen unions. Its studio designs and reproduces special fabrics for the contract market, residential and heritage projects.

The entire collection, stocked in London and displayed in Marvic's Chelsea Harbour showroom and in Rue du Mail, Paris, is also distributed throughout Europe and in twelve showrooms in the US. Samples and cuttings are available to both the trade and the public. The photograph (right) shows 'Patchwork Prints' by Henrietta Spencer-Churchill for Marvic Textiles Ltd.

Unit 1, Westpoint Trading Estate, Alliance Road, Acton, London W3 0RA
tel: 0181 993 0127
fax: 0181 993 1484

US contact:
tel: 212 362 8288

# DESIGN DIRECTORY

## OSBORNE & LITTLE

Osborne & Little's unusually broad approach ranges over a variety of design styles both classic and contemporary in a wide perspective that favours unusual combinations and an extensive palette. Shared colour and design concepts allow fabric and wallpaper co-ordination and each collection builds on the past, providing a continuity that is infused by fresh ideas. Comprehensive ranges include prints, wovens, sheers, silks, trimmings, wallpapers and vinyls. The fabric and wallpaper designs of British designer Nina Campbell and the collections from Liberty Furnishings are now also part of the group.

49 Temperley Road,
London SW12 8QE
tel: 0181 675 2255
fax: 0181 673 8254

US contact:
Osborne & Little Inc.
90 Commerce Road,
Stamford, CT 06902
tel: 203 359 1500

## SCHUMACHER

Schumacher is an American company, distributed in the UK by Turnell & Gigon Ltd. Their Historic Natchez Collection is based on the romance of the quiet southern town of Natchez, Mississippi, with its wealth of opulent and architecturally significant houses. In total, the Historic Natchez Collection includes twelve fabric designs, printed and woven, twelve wallcoverings and three borders available in several colourways.

UK distribution:
Turnell & Gigon Ltd
Chelsea Harbour Design Centre
London SW10 0XE
tel: 0171 351 5142
fax: 0171 376 7945

US contact:
Schumacher
79 Madison Avenue,
New York NY 10016
tel: 212 213 7900

## ZIMMER + ROHDE U.K. LTD

Zimmer + Rohde offers over 3,000 designs and colourways in an adaptable style from contemporary to classic and even

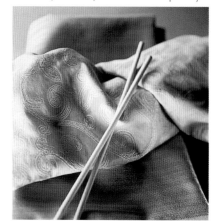

traditional. They specialize in a wealth of plain textures, weaves and sumptuous silks.

15 Chelsea Harbour
Design Centre,
London SW10 0XE
tel: 0171 351 7115
fax: 0171 351 5661

US contact:
Zimmer + Rohde USA,
D & D Building, 979 Third
Avenue, Suite 1616,
New York NY 10022
tel: 212 758 5357

## ZOFFANY

Zoffany specializes in reproducing wallpapers and furnishing fabrics in the handprinted style of the 18th and 19th centuries, with most of their designs and patterns coming from their own exclusive archives. Zoffany focuses on reproducing original material, and adapting decorative themes from the great houses of continental Europe.

As craftsmen printers they are responsible for selecting their own papers, mixing their colours, and controlling their manufacturing. They also offer a special colour printing service, which can be used by independent professional decorators and international designers. Their products, which also include fabrics and carpets, are available through Zoffany outlets and specialist retailers worldwide.

63 South Audley Street,
London W1Y 5BF
tel: 0171 495 2505
fax: 0171 493 7257

US contact:
Whittaker & Woods
5100 Highlands
Parkway, Smyrna,
Atlanta
GA 30082
tel: 800 395 8760

## WALL AND FLOOR FINISHES

### AGORA LONDON

*flooring and finishes*

Agora produces custom-made french parquet, limestone and terracotta floors and period wall panelling. Their parquet and strip floors are made using reclaimed 18th– and 19th–century oak beams or floor boards. Each panel is handmade by highly skilled French craftsmen working in the tradition of the great chateaux. Agora creates marquetry floors and borders using specialist woods, such as birch, ebony and mahogany.

Everything Agora produces is specially designed using classical or original patterns, combining antique materials and the highest level of traditional French craftsmanship, to make some of the finest wall panelling and flooring in the world, available worldwide.

123 Hurlingham Road,
London SW6 3NJ
tel: 0171 731 6327
fax: 0171 736 3573

### KNIGHTSBRIDGE PARQUET COMPANY

*flooring and finishes*

The Knightsbridge Parquet Company specializes in the supply and installation of patterned parquet flooring. Their range of solid woods for both custom-made and standard patterns is broad and special designs to meet customers' needs are also developed at no extra cost.

They offer advice on materials, installation and sub-floor preparation and use a team of highly skilled floor layers.

The Knightsbridge Parquet Company works with both private clients and professional designers and were pleased to design and install the traditional parquet flooring for Victoria Waymouth at The Design House, Cambridge Gate.

49 Herrongate Close, Enfield, Middlesex EN1 3BN
tel/fax: 0181 364 6404

### G.R. PEARCE, FRENCH POLISHING AND WOOD FINISHING SPECIALISTS

*french polishing*

Specialist french polishing contractors, G.R. Pearce is engaged on high-quality contracts throughout the UK and overseas. Traditional hand french polishing and contemporary wood finishing is undertaken by experienced, reliable craftsmen, and ageing new floors and panelling is a speciality. Their work includes a commission by Joanna Wood for The Design House, Cambridge Gate. Technical advice and the preparation of colour/finish samples are also provided by the company.

5 Acton Drive,
Middleton-on-Sea,
West Sussex
PO22 6NA
tel: 01243 583 272
fax: 01243 584 926

### ATTICA

*limestone flooring*

Attica specializes in rare and antique limestone, wood-fired and antique terracotta, handpainted tiles and traditional mosaics.

Sourced from specialist quarries across the globe or handcrafted using traditional methods, products are chosen to provide quality, detail, atmosphere and history in interiors.

As consultants they guide customers through an extensive product library, explain the advantages of different materials and combine them to fit specific needs.

As artists and craftsmen, they will design, produce and install individual custom-made pieces to fit the customers' requirements.

543 Battersea Park Road,
London SW11 3BL
tel: 0171 738 1234
fax: 0171 924 7875
web site: attica.co.uk

# DESIGN DIRECTORY

## VITRUVIUS LIMITED

*marble and stonework*

Vitruvius is a manufacturers of all forms of marble, granite and natural stone – from a simple vanity top or entrance hall floor to the most complex pietre dure panel. All work is on a commission-only basis, and is supported by a full design and installation service.

Unit 20, Ransomes Dock, 35/37 Parkgate Road, London SW11 4NP tel: 0171 223 8209  fax: 0171 924 3045

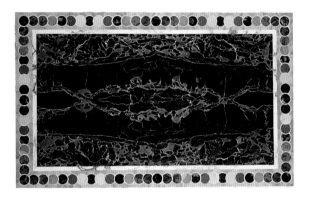

## ZARKA MARBLE

*marble and stonework*

The team at Zarka Marble includes members of the Guild of Master Craftsmen. Marbles, granites, limestones, slates and most commercially available stone can be fashioned into quality kitchen and bathroom surfaces, furniture or any commissioned design.

Zarka Marble will arrange installation or they can supply the cut items worldwide.

41a Belsize Lane,
London
NW3 5AU
tel: 0171 431 3042
fax: 0171 431 3879

room design by GA
Design International

## DONNA REEVES MOSAICS

*mosaic and tiles*

Now London-based, but originally trained in Ravenna, Italy, Donna Reeves' style reflects the earliest styles and techniques employed by Italian craftsmen.

Commissioned works range from floors, borders, walls and splashbacks to wall hangings, and past work for interior designers, architects and private clients has included public art, company logos, restaurant interiors and private homes. Accomplished in a variety of materials: marble, vitreous glass, smalti, ceramics and pebbles, Donna Reeves offers a complete service from design to installation.

33a Kay Road, Clapham, North London SW9 9DF
tel: 0171 733 7060  fax: 01992 421 129

## FOCUS CERAMICS LTD

*mosaic and tiles*

Focus Ceramics Ltd. has been in ceramic tiles, natural stone, associated products such as conglomerate marble, mosaic and glass blocks for decades and have always been known for their quality, reliability, service and friendly, knowledgeable sales team.

Their latest foray into unusual products has been glass tiles in both mosaic and larger formats, as illustrated below, on the floor in the kitchen at The Design House, Cambridge Gate.

Unit 4, Hamm Moor
Lane, Weybridge
Trading Estate,
Weybridge, Surrey
KT15 2SD
tel: 01932 854 881
fax: 01932 851 494
e-mail: focus@dial.
pipex.com web site:
www.info.co.uk/focus/

## DAVIES KEELING TROWBRIDGE LTD

*muralists and specialist decorators*

DKT undertakes projects worldwide, often incorporating items such as the ceiling canvasses photographed below, produced in their studios for subsequent installation on site. Their in-house expertise encompasses paint effects, faux finishes, specialist plasters, gilding, mosaics and murals.

3 Charterhouse Works, Eltringham Street, London SW18 1TD
tel: 0181 874 3565  fax: 0181 874 2058

## BARTHOLOMEUS WOVEN CARPETS

*rugs and carpets*

Bartholomeus is a centenary manufacturer of custom-woven carpets and rugs. The company weaves in wool, linen, silk and cotton to make unique and natural-looking carpets.

FBZ Bartholomeus,
BVBA Nieuwstraat 58,
8820 Torhout,
Belgium
tel: 50 21 22 27
fax: 50 21 38 56

## BOSANQUET IVES LIMITED

*rugs and carpets*

Bosanquet Ives Limited is a specialist supplier of floor coverings to interior decorators, architects and designers.

They are agents for Tai Ping handtufted carpets (photographed below) and stock a comprehensive range of top quality

'Renaissance' Aubusson and Savonnerie rugs, all of which are manufactured from the original documents. Also available is their own range of exclusive Brussels-weave and velvet Wiltons in five widths up to two metres that can be customized to any design at no extra cost. Bosanquet Ives have an ongoing new-product development programme, including a new range of flat weaves in unusual and interesting designs.

3 Court Lodge, 48 Sloane Square, London SW1W 8AT
tel: 0171 730 6241  fax: 0171 730 5341

## CHRISTINE VAN DER HURD

*rugs and carpets*

Beautifully sculpted, coloured, handtufted rugs in 100% New Zealand wool have established Christine Van Der Hurd as one of the most exciting and respected designers of contemporary and classic carpeting.

The company produces custom flooring solutions for clients worldwide. Handtufted and machine-woven (broadloom) carpets are individually designed, sized and produced. Colours are dyed to order from a huge palette.

2/17 Chelsea Harbour Design Centre, London SW10 0XE
tel: 0171 351 6332  fax: 0171 376 3574

US contact:
Christine
Van Der
Hurd
102
Wooster
Street,
New York
NY 10012
tel: 212
343 9070

## DANIELLE HARTWRIGHT

*rugs and carpets*

Danielle Hartwright and Nick Hartwright supply beautiful decorative and antique textiles, carpets and tapestries of the highest quality, be they antique pieces, such as Agra, Savonnerie and Zeigler, or their handmade reproduction carpets for leading designers and architects.

Working with traditional craftsmen, they produce carpets that retain the quality of antique rugs in weave and technique, recapturing the traditional designs and colouration of priceless antique carpets at affordable costs. Danielle oversees each project

personally and works closely with Victoria Waymouth, including designing and supplying carpets for the restoration of Goodwood House.

Cassallena, Chalfont Lane, West Hyde, Rickmansworth, Herts WD3 2XN
tel: 01895 824 137/ 01494 875 546
fax: 01895 824 150/ 01494 870 038

## RANKINS (GLASS) COMPANY LTD

*Specialist glass and glazing*

Rankins supplied and fitted black and white Colorline wall-lining glass and decorative mirrors in the bathrooms designed by Stephen Ryan. These products as well as a substantial selection of other unusual and standard glasses are available from their product range.

The original company was formed in 1880, making it one of the oldest independents in the UK, and offers old-fashioned service with innovative technological advances in the art of glass. Their service includes design and installation facilities as well as a full technical advisory service.

The London Glass Centre, 24-34 Pearson Street, London E2 8JD
tel: 0171 729 4200
fax: 0171 729 7135/9197

photographer: Nick Carter of Southampton

## STOCKWELL RUGS & CARPETS

*rugs and carpets*

Specialists in the design and supply of luxury handmade carpets to order, Stockwell Rugs & Carpets creates unique carpets and rugs through their London-based design studio and are renowned for the quality of their design work.

Rugs and carpets can be supplied in handknotted, handtufted or 'Aubusson'-styles. Commissions include The Royal Pavilion, Brighton, The State Capitol Building, Utah, The Governor's

Mansion, Puerto Rico and numerous international residences and super yachts and planes.

24 Harcourt Street, London W1H 1DT
tel: 0171 224 8380
fax: 0171 224 8381

US contact: Stockwell Carpets (USA Ltd)
tel: 860 889 2880

## CAROLYN BENSON

*specialist paint effects*

Carolyn Benson is a specialist painter who simulates any style of classical ornamentation using traditional recipes, from inlaid woods and stones to adapting complex designs to plain walls. She also works with plaster and leather, and paints fabrics. She is trained as a restorer, which has given her a developed eye for colour, and her work is understated. She has worked worldwide for private clients and the public sector, with architects and interior designers,

and has recently helped with the restoration of Goodwood House with Victoria Waymouth, with whom she works closely.

21 Streatley Road, London NW6 7LJ
tel/fax: 0171 624 1894

## CELIA MINOPRIO DECORATIVE PAINTER

*specialist paint effects*

Celia Minoprio has worked as an innovative specialist painter in Italy for the past fifteen years and has recently launched her

company in London. Her specialist finishes range from early Italian Renaissance techniques to contemporary murals, polished plaster and gilding.

Celia works all over the world and has undertaken projects in palaces, hotels, town houses and bedsitting rooms. Her training in fine art has helped her to develop finishes such as marble, neo-classical motifs (the photograph above shows a neo-classical, gilded panel design) and personalized imagery that includes portraits of pets.

161 Sullivan Court, Broomhouse Lane, London SW6 3DN
tel: 0171 736 0236

## MAECENAS RESTORATION AND DECORATION

*specialist paint effects*

Specialists in painted and gilt finishes on walls, leather and wallpaper, with training in restoration of painted and gilt antique furniture. They offer personalized service, from the more simple paint finishes required in today's private houses or hotels to the complete design and painting of elaborate schemes required for more imposing rooms in large stately homes.

13 Crescent Place,
London SW3 2EA
tel: 0171 581 1083
fax: 0171 584 5150

photographer: Joshua Brigg

## *ARCHITECTURAL ELEMENTS*

## CROWTHER OF SYON LODGE

*period panelling*

Syon Lodge is home to what is now the oldest architectural antiques business in Britain.

A major part of the company's business is the work of a team of skilled craftsmen on the restoration of antique panelled rooms. The team also designs and manufactures period-style panelling, using solid antique timbers, and installs them anywhere in the world.

Syon Lodge,
Busch Corner,
London Road,
Isleworth, Middlesex
TW7 5BH
tel: 0181 560 7978
fax: 0181 568 7572
e-mail: crowther.syon–
lodge@virgin.net
web site: www.
crowther–syon–lodge.
co.uk

## HAYLES & HOWE LIMITED

*plasterwork*

Hayles & Howe is recognized as the leading company involved in the restoration and conservation of plasterwork in historic and listed buildings. They also specialize in the restoration of scagliola, and can help architects in the design and construction of ornate ceilings in any shape or size.

Picton House, 25 Picton Street,
Montpelier, Bristol BS6 5PZ
tel: 0117 924 6673   fax: 0117 924 3928
e-mail: 106066.1614@compuserve.com

US contact: Hayles & Howe, Inc.
3500 Parkdale Avenue, Bldg 1 West, Ground Floor,
Baltimore MD 21211
tel: 410 462 0986
e-mail: handh@charm.net

photographer: Bob Whitfield

# DESIGN DIRECTORY

## LIGHTING

### CUBE LIGHTING & INDUSTRIAL DESIGNS LTD

Cube Lighting designs and manufactures contemporary custom-made luminaires for both commercial and domestic projects. Working from clients' concepts or offering a full conceptual design and manufacturing service, Cube can supply individually designed products tailored to specific environments.

They offer an innovative standard product range, utilizing the latest lamp technology including: darklight and indirect downlights, wiresystems, low-voltage and discharge recessed uplights, including the revolutionary 'Beacon' which converts from a flush

uplight to a low-level sidelight or bollard within seconds.

Products are manufactured and finished in workshops in the UK. The company ships to clients worldwide.

The Bothy Mentmore,
Nr Leighton Buzzard,
Buckinghamshire LU7 0QG
tel/fax: 01296 661 853

### JOHN CULLEN LIGHTING

John Cullen Lighting has helped transform houses and gardens all over the world. A unique collection of low-voltage fittings offers creative lighting effects, discreet appearance, performance and good design. A site visit or showroom consultation can be arranged for design ideas and advice from staff trained to find the most appropriate lighting solutions.

585 Kings Road London
SW6 2EH
tel: 0171 371 5400
fax: 0171 371 7799
e-mail:
jcl@dial.pipex.com

### RENWICK & CLARKE

Renwick & Clarke supply beautiful lighting, furniture and decorative accessories, chosen for their craftsmanship, taste and element of fun.

The extensive lighting range includes lampshades, lampbases, chandeliers, wall lights, lanterns, vanity lights and the Niermann Weeks collection.

Lampshades are handmade in silk and luxurious devoré velvet. Lampbases are available in handfinished porcelain as well as handpainted, and also wood finishes.

190 Ebury Street, London
SW1W 8UP
tel: 0171 730 8913
fax: 0171 730 4508

### THE LIGHT STORE

The Light Store specializes in all types of lighting and also offers a design and installation service.

They have a wide range of lighting from traditional to modern, imported from all over the world, and will manufacture custom-made fittings. The Light Store also specializes in exterior lighting and has a wide range of fittings.

The Light Store has completed commissions in Europe, USA and the Middle East.

11 Clifton Road,
Maida Vale,
London
W9 1SZ
tel: 0171 286 8033
fax: 0171 286 8133
email: 113211-3156@compuserve.com

## BEDROOM AND BATHROOM

### BATHROOMS INTERNATIONAL LTD

*bathrooms*

The UK and Middle East distributor for the THG/JCD range of bathroom taps, showers, accessories, baths and sanitaryware, their unique products are considered the finest in the world, with 136 tap and waterfall spout ranges available in 70 standard finishes from the simplest chrome to semi-precious stones or crystals. Baths and basins are available in 150 plain colours or mother of pearl with unique decoration. Considered the jewellers of their

industry, their products grace palaces, yachts, hotels and private residences worldwide.

54 The Burroughs,
London,
NW4 4AN
tel: 0181
202 1002
fax: 0181
202 6439

US contact:
through UK office
photographer:
Joshua Briggs

### VOLA

*bathrooms*

Vola's classical range of kitchen and bathroom brassware by Arne Jacobsen and glass bowls by Vitra Form can be combined to produce the ultimate in bathroom chic.

Vola offers a complete selection of kitchen, bathroom and shower fittings as well as a complementary range of accessories. Glass basins are available in a variety of styles and colours.

Unit 12,
Ampthill Business Park,
Station Road,
Ampthill, Bedfordshire
MK45 2QW
tel: 01525 841 155
fax: 01525 841 177

US contact: Kroin Inc. USA
tel: 617 492 4000

### MONOGRAMMED LINEN SHOP

*bedrooms*

The Monogrammed Linen Shop specializes in embroidered linens for the entire house. They take pride in using the finest cottons and linens and stock a wide selection of exclusive designs.

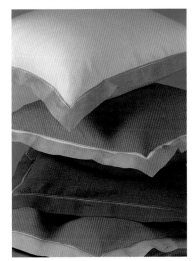

They will make up any design to match specific decorating schemes. They also carry bathroom accessories, scented sachets and candles, night wear, and cashmere and wool throws, and have an in-house monogramming service.

168 Walton Street,
London
SW3 2JL
tel: 0171 589 4033
fax: 0171 823 7745

### PRATESI LINENS

*bedrooms*

The Pratesi reputation is founded upon the quality of their materials and a commitment to aesthetic pleasure. The finest Egyptian cotton, angel-skin percale, jacquards, linens, silks and Mongolian cashmere are used throughout their collection of bed, bath and table linens.

1/2 Chelsea Harbour Design Centre, London SW10 0XE
tel: 0171 349 0090
fax: 0171 349 0035.

US contact:
829 Madison Avenue,
New York NY 10021
tel: 212 288 2315

# DESIGN DIRECTORY

## *FURNITURE*

### B & T ANTIQUES

*antique furniture*

Bernadette Lewis, born and bred in France, has an innate appreciation of the French look for which, she says, there is an increasing demand. Her shop reflects this image, and she does not confine her stock to a particular style or period. Be it an armoire or Meridienne for the boudoir, a commode for the drawing room or a simple piece for the kitchen or conservatory, if it is not in stock, she nearly always will be successful in finding it.

79–81 Ledbury Road, London W11 2AG
tel: 0171 229 7001
fax: 0171 229 2031

### HRW ANTIQUES

*antique furniture*

HRW Antiques is a wholesale and retail operation with extensive showrooms in west London and a retail operation at Fortnum & Mason.

The varied stock dates from the early 18th century to the late 19th century and includes traditional English furniture, continental and provincial items, decorative objects and a selection of pictures, prints and watercolours.

HRW Antiques has an international clientele and works widely in Europe, America, the Far East and the Middle East.

26 Sulivan Road
London SW6 3DT
tel: 0171 371 7995
fax: 0171 371 9522

### ARCHER & SMITH LTD

*custom-made furniture*

Archer & Smith are makers of high-quality furniture and specialized joinery, working closely with leading architects, designers, decorators and retailers and using the finest quality materials.

They produce both traditional and contemporary styles of furniture using modern technology only when it offers a superior standard to time-honoured traditional methods. Each piece of furniture is individually handmade to the exact requirements of each client.

The Manor House, Hodson Road, Chiseldon, Swindon, Wiltshire SN4 0LN
tel: 01793 740 375  fax: 01793 741 110

e-mail: asmith740@aol.com
web site: http:// members.aol.com/ asmith740/

US contact:
Elijah Slocum
tel: 800 310 8011
e-mail: EliSlocum@aol.com

### DAVID LINLEY FURNITURE LIMITED

*custom-made furniture*

David Linley has an international reputation for custom-made furniture. He applies a fresh, contemporary approach to the production of functional yet aesthetically pleasing wooden furniture and objects, using traditional marquetry techniques and a variety of woods. The company work with clients around the world. Commissions range from the smallest table to an entire panelled room.

David Linley has a shop within Bergdorf Goodman, New York, selling a range of accessories, and has also expanded the showroom in London.

60 Pimlico Road, London SW1 W8LP
tel: 0171 730 7300  fax: 0171 730 8869

## JOHN BILES DESIGN
## (PHOENIX GREEN ANTIQUES)

*custom-made furniture*

Formerly an auctioneer, John Biles opened his own antique shop in 1982. He was soon aware that many present-day needs could not be fulfilled by antique furniture, and began designing and making his own pieces. He works for private clients and interior designers to create individual looks.

The quality of his work can be seen this gilt console table and mirror.

London Road, Phoenix Green, Hartley, Witney, Hampshire RG27 8RT
tel: 01252 844 430  fax: 01252 844 784

## JULIAN STANLEY WOODCARVING –
## FURNITURE

*custom-made furniture*

This workshop recreates and undertakes lavishly carved classical work from the 18th century, fine figure carving, portrait busts, mirror frames and architectural pieces of all dimensions.

Their carefully selected polishers, gilders, painters and upholsters achieve superb standards of finish and quality. Julian Stanley Woodcarving – Furniture also offers a consultancy and design service.

Unit 5,
The Sitch,
Longborough,
Moreton-in-Marsh
Gloucestershire GL56 0QJ
tel/fax: 01451 831 122

## CUSK & WOOD LTD

*fine handpainted furniture*

Cusk & Wood Ltd is a small company specializing in fine hand-painted furniture, mirrors and accessories, upholding traditional European techniques developed in the 18th and 19th centuries. The company has established an international reputation for producing high-quality work, designed and executed by a team of specialist painters in their central London studio.

They undertake commissions for special designs, sizes or finishes. Visitors are welcome in the studio by appointment.

Unit 1, The Quadrangle,
49 Atalanta Street,
London SW6 6TR
tel: 0171 386 9595
fax: 0171 386 9495
e-mail: cuskwood@btinternet.com

## THE STAINTHORPE
## FURNITURE CO LTD

*fine handpainted furniture*

Stainthorpe Furniture is a custom cabinet maker. Their designers and craftsmen have an expert knowledge of furniture and have many years of experience in designing and making free-standing pieces. Their finishes include not only a great variety of woods and veneers but also gilding, painting and laminates. The design team re-interpret past styles using their own creativity to produce stunning, unique pieces for both interior designers and private clientele. Each piece is benchmade in the UK by craftsmen and can be shipped anywhere in the world.

Unit 138,
Battersea Business Centre,
99–109 Lavender Hill,
London SW11 5QL
tel: 0171 801 0095
fax: 0171 350 2249

US contact:
330 North Hamilton Street
High Point, NC 27260
tel: 910 886 7102

# DESIGN DIRECTORY

## ATRIUM

*specialist furniture*

Over the past twenty years, Atrium has developed into a major force supplying modern furniture, lighting and textiles for residential, corporate, hotel and leisure environments. Atrium are UK distributors for prestigious companies such as: B&B Italia, Cassina, Cattelan, Fritz Hansen, Interlubke, Moroso, Novasuede etc.

22 – 24 St. Giles High Street, London WC2H 8LN
tel: 0171 379 7288
fax: 0171 240 2080
e-mail: all@atrivm.co.uk
web site: http://www.atrivm.co.uk

## CAREW–JONES & ASSOCIATES LTD

*specialist furniture*

Established in 1980, Carew–Jones & Associates, with Quadrant 4, design, manufacture and supply the finest Perspex (Plexiglas) and glass furniture.

Clean, classic lines offer effective solutions and co-ordinate perfectly with traditional and contemporary furniture in both corporate and domestic environments. The photograph below shows a 'Redenham'-style console table and coffee table.

188 Walton Street,
London SW3 2JL
tel: 0171 225 2411
fax: 0171 225 2422
e-mail: carewjones@aol.col

## EVOLUTION OFFICE FURNITURE LIMITED

*specialist furniture*

Evolution Office Furniture specializes in beautifully finished modular Swedish furniture for clients who need functional, flexible pieces for the office or home environment. Their Round Office range is the result of over twenty-five years of experience in high quality ergonomically-engineered desk systems, veneered in natural woods.

The Round Office system is based on a round table that can be used in sections or, for maximum work space, supplemented with additional table sections made at various heights. This versatile,

adaptable, modular concept enables their furniture to grow to accommodate filing, drawers and computer work stations.

Glastonbury House,
74a High Street, Billingshurst
West Sussex RH14 9QS
tel: 01403 786 006
fax: 01403 785 775

room design: KLC School of Design
photographer: Nick Carter of Southampton

## THE PARSONS TABLE COMPANY LTD

*specialist furniture*

Parsons Table supply unusual, finely crafted furniture, including a new range of occasional tables, chests of drawers and bedside tables. The collection is handsome, with interesting details not normally associated with reproduction furniture. The company also has a finely made and well-finished selection of French and English chair frames and beds. They can copy almost any chair frame to match an existing model.

362 Fulham Road,
London SW10 9UU
tel: 0171 352 7444
fax: 0171 376 4677

## GARDEN FURNITURE

### LLOYD CHRISTIE

*conservatories and gazebos*

Lloyd Christie designs and manufactures custom-made hardwood conservatories. Constructed with the finest timbers and fittings, each building is designed to harmonize with the character of the property and the personal taste of the client. Lloyd Christie also manufactures a wide range of gazebos, trellis, arbours, rose arches, pergolas and decking. Clients can either design and cost their own trellis scheme or use the company's design service. Gazebos, pergolas,

arbours, rose arches and decking are available in standard sizes or to specification.

1 New Kings Road,
London SW6 4UG
tel: 0171 731 3484
fax: 0171 371 9952
e-mail: lloydchristie@
dial.pipex.com
web site:
www.lloydchristie.com

### ASHTON PRODUCTS

*garden furniture and ornamentation*

Ashton Products specializes in distinctive outdoor furniture, and the Kettal range offers a harmonious combination of modern and traditional styles in teak, aluminium, loom and resin, in a variety of colours and accessory materials. The furniture is suitable for both contract and domestic use.

The Golf teak line features a comprehensive range of chairs, tables, benches and sun-loungers in traditional and contemporary designs.

To complete the furniture, Ashton offers a selection of wood-framed garden umbrellas in a variety of colours and sizes.

Satco House,
Claylands Road,
Bishop's Waltham
Southampton SO32 1BH
tel: 01489 894 666
fax: 01489 896 289

### CROWTHER OF SYON LODGE

*garden furniture and ornamentation*

The Crowther family has dealt in architectural antiques for over 120 years. Syon Lodge holds a remarkable collection of ornament for both the interior and exterior – urns, statues, fountains, seats, animal figures, temples, entrance gates, chimneypieces and panelled rooms. Also displayed is a range of quality contemporary pieces.

Syon Lodge, Busch Corner
London Road, Isleworth
Middlesex TW7 5BH
tel: 0181 560 7978
fax: 0181 568 7572
e-mail: crowther.syon–lodge
@virgin.net
web site: www.crowther–syon–
lodge.co.uk

### SUMMIT FURNITURE, INC.

*garden furniture and ornamentation*

Summit Furniture, Inc. was founded in 1979, initially to manufacture the designs of noted American designer Kipp Stewart. At the heart of all Summit furniture is solid Tectona Grandis teak, a renewable resource grown in Indonesia on certified plantations. Summit furniture is hand-assembled at Summit's factory in Indonesia.

198 Ebury Street,
Orange Square,
London
SW1W 8UN
tel: 0171 259 9244
fax: 0171 259 9246

US contact:
5 Harris Court,
Monterey,
CA 93940
tel: 408 375 7811

# DESIGN DIRECTORY

## *OBJETS D'ART, ANTIQUES AND PAINTINGS*

### IONA ANTIQUES

*art*

Iona Antiques has probably the largest selection of 19th-century animal paintings to be found anywhere. They are regular exhibitors at the major antique shows in New York, San Francisco and Los Angeles in addition to the Grosvenor House and Olympia fairs in London.

PO Box 285, London W8 6HZ
tel: 0171 602 1193
fax: 0171 371 2843
e-mail:info@collectors–on–line.com
web site: http://www.art–on–line.com/iona

### MARILYNNE CAHN & CO.

*art*

Marilynne Cahn & Co. sources and supplies art and artefacts to hotels, residences, offices, restaurants, bars, health clubs, cruise ships – anywhere in the world where pictures are required.

The company work closely with interior designers to supply something unique to the situation and picking up on particular details or culture . An extensive knowledge of the market place enables them to source appropriate art, pictures, mirrors, sculptures, wall hangings and artefacts at the right price for each project. They provide clients with a complete service from selection through to installation.

Heston Court Camp Road, London SW19 4UW
tel: 0181 946 7050
fax: 0181 946 7055
email: MCArt@btinternet.com
photographer: Nicola Clark

### LUCY B. CAMPBELL

*art*

The Lucy B. Campbell gallery specializes in fine 16th- through 19th-century antiquarian prints and paintings. Subjects included in the gallery's varied stock are natural history, botanical, architectural and topographical. Lucy Campbell also represents contemporary artists including the naive artist Anna Pugh and botanical artists Alastair Gordon and Christine F. Stephenson. Services offered by the gallery include fine art restoration and individually designed handmade framing.

123 Kensington Church Street, London W8 7LP
tel: 0171 727 2205
fax: 0171 229 4252
e-mail: lucy.b.campbell@dial.pipex.com

### LALIQUE

*decorative accessories*

Art nouveau interiors inspired René Lalique to design perfume bottles for perfume makers. A finely fluted shell in either clear or opal satin-finished crystal adorns this bottle, and because of its original shape the bottle can also be used as an inkwell.

Lalique also produces art deco and art nouveau crystal ornaments featuring plants, foliage and animals, as well as vases, reliefs, and other accoutrements for the home.

201 Sloane Street, London SW1 X9QX
tel: 0171 245 9090

## RENWICK & CLARKE

*decorative accessories*

Renwick & Clarke supplies beautiful lighting, furniture and decorative accessories, chosen for their craftsmanship, taste and element of fun.

The range of decorative accessories is extensive and includes fine porcelain and china dinnerware, decorative china and creamware, silver, pewter and glass. A particular, exclusive line is custom-coloured, embossed and gilded leather panels.

190 Ebury Street, London SW1W 8UP
tel: 0171 730 8913
fax: 0171 730 4508

## GHISLAINE STEWART DESIGNS

*door handles and lamps*

Ghislaine Stewart Designs produces a range of contemporary classic door furniture, lamps and fireplaces. The door furniture is available in bronze (using the lost-wax method of casting) or exotic hardwoods. The lamps are made in a variety of materials including bronze, leather and silver. Fireplaces are in stone and bronze. All the bronze work can be finished to customers' specification and can be patinated in a range of colours, or plated. GSD undertakes special commissions. All products are finished by hand.

110 Fentiman Road, London
SW8 1QA
tel/fax: 0171 820 9440

US contact:
Alison Rankin, Pemberley Inc.
tel: 440 423 1830

## MCKINNEY & CO

*finials and curtain poles*

McKinney & Co is recognized as one of the leading specialists in curtain poles, finials and accessories. Traditional methods are used with metal and glass to give a more modern look when required. Special commissions are welcome and all finishes are customized to allow for individual looks.

Studio P, The Old Imperial Laundry, 71 Warriner Gardens, London SW11 4XW
tel: 0171 627 5077
fax: 0171 627 5088

US contact:
Christopher Hyland Inc., D & D Building, Suite 1714, 979 Third Avenue, New York NY 10022
tel: 212 688 6121

## CLASSIC BINDINGS

*library books*

Classic Bindings is one of the leading suppliers of decorative antiquarian books worldwide. They provide a total service ranging from individual volumes to complete libraries, and have a client base that includes interior designers, architects and antique dealers as well as their private clients. Their varied stock range includes fine and illustrated collectible books, decorative bindings and library objects and furniture.

61 Cambridge Street, Pimlico, London, SW1V 4PS
tel: 0171 834 5554
fax: 0171 630 6632
e-mail: info@ classicbindings. net
web site: www. classicbindings. net

# ACKNOWLEDGEMENTS

PHOTO CREDITS

1, Joshua Briggs; 3, Nick Carter of Southampton, 5, Alberto Piovano
Introduction 6, courtesy of Cambridge Gate Management; 7 (above), courtesy of Sibyl Colefax & John Fowler; 7 (below), 9 (below), 10 (right), 11 (right) Joshua Briggs courtesy of IDH Ltd; 8 (below), Joshua Briggs courtesy of Wendy Cushing Trimmings; 8 (top), courtesy of Christophe Gollut; 8 (middle), courtesy of Charles Rutherfoord; 9 (top), courtesy of Charles Bateson Design Consultants; 9 (middle), Kerry Kennedy courtesy of Percheron; 10 (left), 11 (left), courtesy of Clifton Interiors.
The Classic Look 12 left © Henrietta Spencer-Churchill; 12 right Peter Aprahamian courtesy of House & Garden; 13 above, below left courtesy of Joanna Trading; 13 below right Nick Carter courtesy of IDH Ltd.
Henrietta Spencer-Churchill All photographs © Henrietta Spencer-Churchill
Victoria Waymouth 26 and 27, Peter Hodsoll; 29, 30 and 31 (above) Nick Carter, courtesy of IDH Ltd.; 31 (below right), 35 Mark Luscombe-Whyte; 32, 33 and 37 (above), Mark Luscombe-Whyte, courtesy of Country Homes & Interiors; 34, James Mortimer, courtesy of Victoria Waymouth Interiors; 36, 37 (below) James Mortimer.
Lavinia Dargie 38, 40, 41, 42, 43 (top two), Peter Aprahamian, courtesy of Dargie Lewis Designs Ltd.; 46 (above right) Peter Aprahamian, courtesy of House & Garden; 39 and 47 (below), Michael Maule, courtesy of Dargie Lewis Designs Ltd; 43 (below), 44 Andreas von Einsiedel; 45 (above), 46 (above left and three below) D & R Ward; 45 (below) and 47 (above) John Cumings, courtesy of Cartier.
Joanna Wood 50 (below), courtesy of Cambridge Gate Management. All other photographs courtesy of Joanna Trading.
Eclecticism 58 above and below right Peter Aprahamian courtesy of Alidad Ltd; 58 left and below right Fritz von der Schulenburg; 59 above James Mortimer courtesy of The World of Interiors; 59 below Joshua Briggs.
Tessa Kennedy 61 (above right), 65 (above), 67 (left), 70 (below) Joshua Briggs. All other photographs Fritz von der Schulenburg.
Christophe Gollut 72, 79 and 80, James Mortimer, courtesy of The World Of Interiors; 73 and 83, courtesy of Christopher Gollut; 74, 76 and 77, Joshua Briggs, courtesy of IDH Ltd.; 81, Arabella Ashley, courtesy of IDH Ltd.; 82, Fritz von der Schulenburg.

Alidad All photographs Peter Aprahamian, courtesy of Alidad Ltd.
Colourful Modernism 96 left Guy Hills © William Peter Kosmas 1998; 96 right Alberto Piovano; 97 above Jerome Darblay; 97 left and right Tim Beddow.
Jenny Armit 98,99,100,101, 108 (top two) and 109 Joshua Briggs courtesy of Jenny Armit Interiors; 102, 103, 104 and 107 Tim Beddow; 105 Clive Frost courtesy of Jenny Armit Interiors; 106, courtesy of Jenny Armit Interiors; 108 (below) courtesy of Agenda.
Philip Hooper 118 and 119 Trevor Richards, courtesy of Country Homes & Interiors; 110, 111, 112 and 113, Guy Hills, courtesy of Philip Hooper Designer Associates Ltd.; 114, 115, 116, 117, 120 and 121 Guy Hills © Willam Peter Kosmas.
Charles Rutherfoord 122, 123, 128 (right), 132 (below left) and 133 Judy Goldhill; 124 and 125, Joshua Briggs; 126 and 127 David Bache; 128 (left), 129 (left), 130, 131 (below left), 132 (above middle), Jerome Darblay; 129 (right) courtesy of Schoner Wohnen; 131 (above) Andreas von Einsiedel; 131 (below right), 132 (above right) Alberto Piovano; 132 (above left, below right), Tom Leighton.
Contemporary Architectural 134 left Nick Carter of Southampton; 134 right James Mortimer courtesy of The World of Interiors; 135 above left Peter Wadley; 135 above right Henry Wilson; 135 below Joshua Briggs courtesy of IDH Ltd.
Baker Nevile 136, 137 138 and 139, Andreas von Einsiedel; 140, Mike Frost; 141 and 142, Tim Goffe, courtesy of Country Homes & Interiors; 143 (main picture), June Buck, courtesy of Country Life; 143 (below) courtesy of Baker Nevile; 144 and 145, Tom Leighton; 146 and 147, James Mortimer, courtesy of The World Of Interiors; 148 and 149, Joshua Briggs, courtesy of IDH Ltd.
Peter Wadley 150, 151, 152 and 153 Nick Carter of Southampton; 154, 155, 156, 157, 158 and 159, 160 (above right, below left and right) and 161 Peter Wadley; 160 (above left and middle), Antoine Raffoul.
Stephen Ryan 162 and 164, Henry Wilson; 163, 167, 169 and 172 (all of first column), John Spragg; 165, 166 and 171 Arabella Ashley, courtesy of IDH Ltd.; 168 and 170 Joshua Briggs, courtesy of IDH Ltd.; 172 (below right), courtesy of Stephen Ryan Design & Decoration.

DESIGNERS' ADDRESSES

Lady Henrietta Spencer-Churchill IIDA IDDA
Woodstock Designs
26 Sulivan Road, London SW6 3DX
Tel: 0171 731 8399 Fax: 0171 731 8856
and
7 High Street, Woodstock, Oxfordshire OX20 1TE
Tel: 01993 811887 Fax: 01993 813487

Lady Victoria Waymouth IIDA
Victoria Waymouth Interiors
30 Old Church Street, London SW3 5BX
Tel: 0171 376 5244 Fax: 0171 351 3927

Lavinia Dargie IIDA IDDA
Dargie Lewis Designs Ltd
5 Napier Avenue, London SW6 3PS
Tel: 0171 736 3225 Fax: 0171 371 5885
E-Mail: dargie@dargielewis.demon.co.uk

Joanna Wood IIDA IDDA
Joanna Trading
7 Bunhouse Place, London SW1W 8HU
Tel: 0171 730 0693 Fax: 0171 730 4135
E-Mail: Joannaw@joannawood.com
Web site: www.joannawood.com

Tessa Kennedy IIDA
Tessa Kennedy Design Ltd
Studio 5, 91-97 Freston Road, London W11 4BD
Tel: 0171 221 4546 Fax: 0171 229 2899
E-Mail: TKDESIGN@compuserve.com

Christophe Gollut IIDA
116 Fulham Road, London SW3 6HU
Tel: 0171 370 4101 Fax: 0171 370 4123

Alidad IIDA
Studio 4, The William Blake House, Bridge Lane,
London SW11 3AD
Tel: 0171 924 3033 Fax: 0171 923 3088
E-Mail: alidad@alidad.demon.co.uk

Jenny Armit IIDA
Jenny Armit Interiors Ltd
167 Westbourne Grove, London W11 2RS
Tel: 0171 243 1606 Fax: 0171 792 3406
Los Angeles, USA tel: 213 500 3204
E-Mail: jennyarmit@compuserve.com

Philip Hooper IIDA
Philip Hooper Design Associates
Studio 30, The Old Latchmere School,
38 Burns Road, London SW11 5GY
Tel: 0171 978 6662 Fax: 0171 223 3713
E-Mail: jlad@netcomuk.co.uk

Charles Rutherfoord MCSD
51 The Chase, London SW4 0NP
Tel: 0171 627 0182 Fax: 0171 720 0799

Christopher Nevile IIDA
Baker Nevile Design Partnership
7 Barlow Place, Off Bruton Lane, London, W1X 7AE
Tel: 0171 491 9900 Fax: 0171 491 9919

Peter Wadley MA Dip. Arch. (Cantab) RIBA
Peter Wadley Architects
31 Fentiman Road, London SW8 1LD
Tel: 0171 735 3875 Fax: 0171 793 7667

Stephen Ryan IIDA IDDA
Stephen Ryan Design & Decoration
7 Clarendon Cross, London W11 4AP
Tel: 0171 243 0864 Fax: 0171 243 3151
E-Mail: SRyanDesign@compuserve.com

The International Interior Design Association (IIDA)
International Headquarters
341 Merchandise Mart, Chicago, Illinois
60654-1104 USA
Tel: (312) 467 1950 Fax: (312) 467 0779

The International Interior Design Association (IIDA) UK chapter
Phoenix House, 86 Fulham High Street,
London SW6 3LF
Tel: 0171 384 2414 Fax: 0171 384 2454

Interior Decorators and Designers Association (IDDA)
1/4 Chelsea Harbour Design Centre, Chelsea Harbour, Lots Road, London SW10 0XE
Tel: 0171 349 0800 Fax: 0171 349 0500

AUTHORS' ACKNOWLEDGEMENTS

Particular thanks to all the designers represented in this book who have talked at length about their design philosophies and projects. Thanks also to all the photographers who have provided material, in particular Andreas von Einsiedel, Nick Carter of Southampton and Fritz von der Schulenburg. With grateful thanks to Neil Powling and the directors of Cambridge Gate Limited, The Conservation Practice and Balfour Beatty for their respective roles in the creation of The British Interior Design Exhibition 1997.

Special thanks to Cindy Richards for her creativity and enthusiasm, Alex Parsons and Kate Yeates for their editing, Christine Wood for her design and Muna Reyal for all her help.

# INDEX

# INDEX